VOCAL SHEET MUSIC

POP HITS

ISBN 978-1-5400-1512-9

HAL•LEONARD®

Visit Hal Leonard Online at
www.halleonard.com

Contact Us:
Hal Leonard
7777 West Bluemound Road
Milwaukee, WI 53213
Email: info@halleonard.com

In Europe contact:
Hal Leonard Europe Limited
42 Wigmore Street
Marylebone, London, W1U 2RN
Email: info@halleonardeurope.com

In Australia contact:
Hal Leonard Australia Pty. Ltd.
4 Lentara Court
Cheltenham, Victoria, 3192 Australia
Email: info@halleonard.com.au

ALL OF ME

Words and Music by JOHN STEPHENS
and TOBY GAD

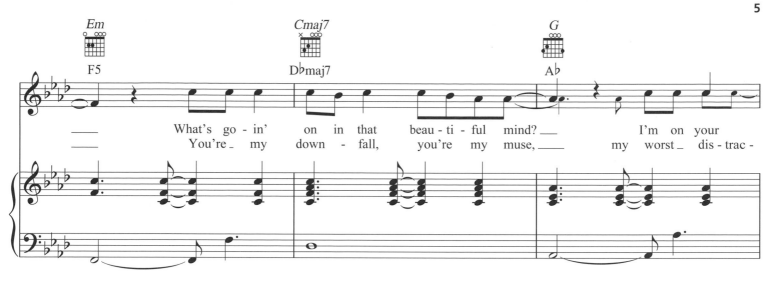

What's go-in' on in that beau-ti-ful mind? ___ I'm on your

You're ___ my down-fall, you're my muse, ___ my worst ___ dis-trac-

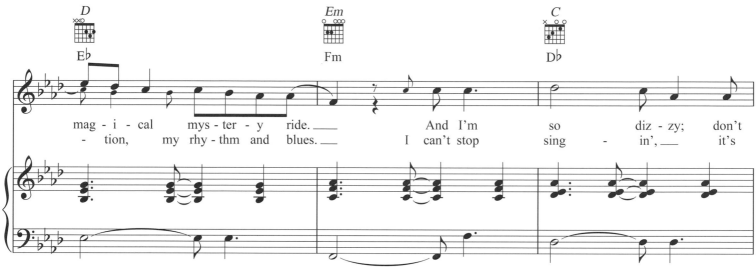

mag-i-cal mys-ter-y ride. ___ And I'm so diz-zy; don't

-tion, my rhy-thm and blues. ___ I can't stop sing - in', ___ it's

know what hit me. But I'll be al - right. }

ring - in' in ___ my head ___ for you. ___ } My

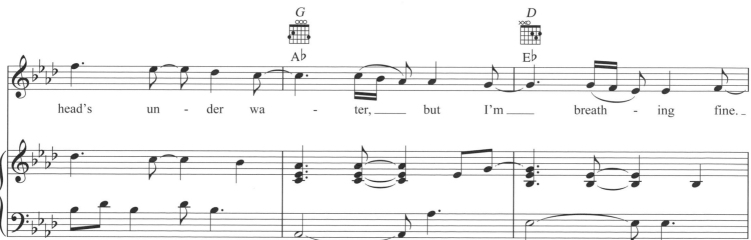

head's un-der wa - ter, ___ but I'm ___ breath - ing fine. ___

You're ___ cra - zy and I'm ___ out ___ of my mind. ___

'Cause all of me ___ loves

all of you. ___ Love your curves and all your edg -

es, all your per - fect im - per - fec - tions. Give your

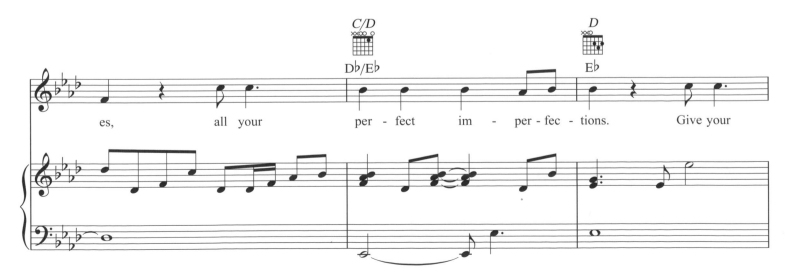

APOLOGIZE

Words and Music by
RYAN TEDDER

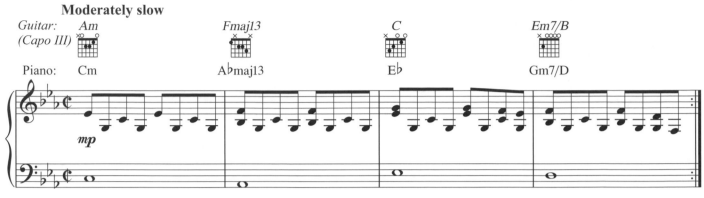

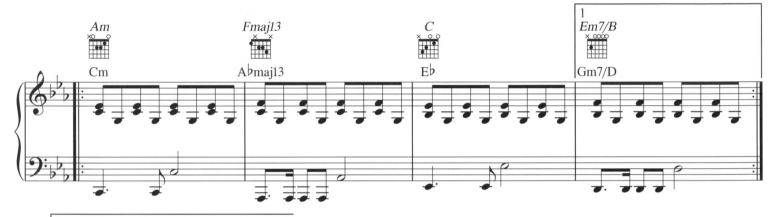

I'm hold-in' on your rope, got me ten feet off the ground.

And I'm hear-in' what you say, __ but I

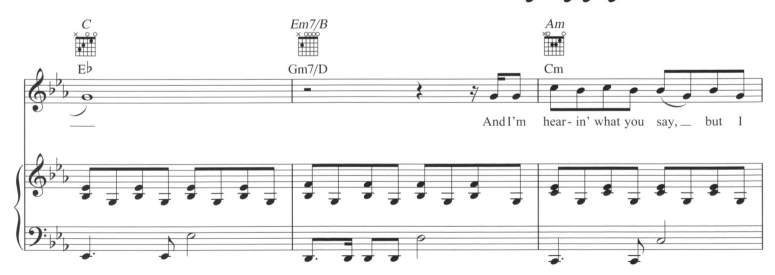

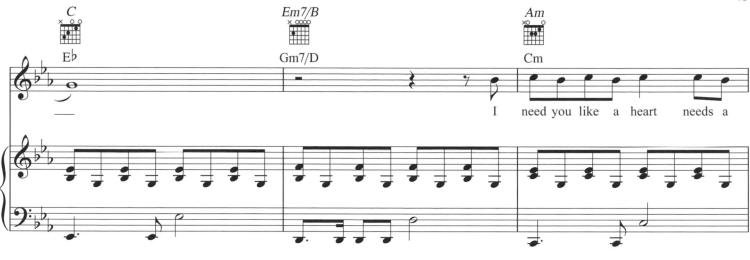

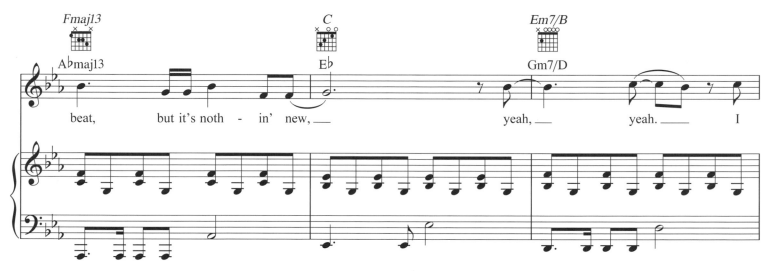

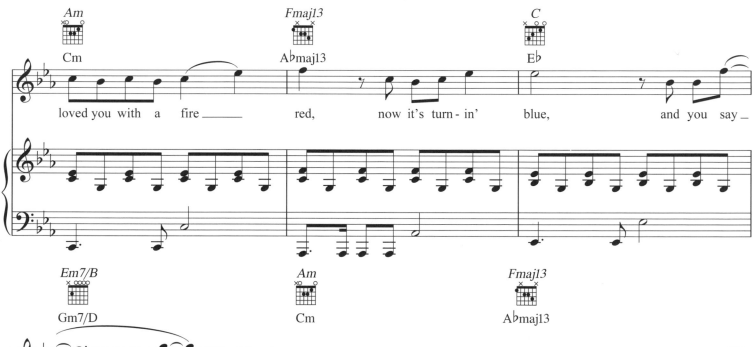

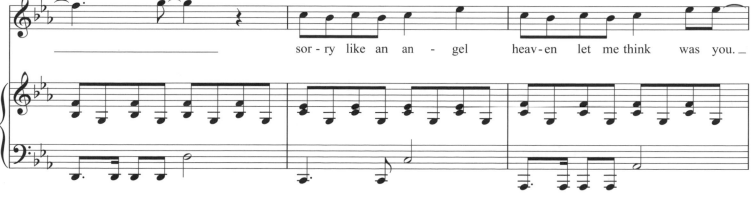

BREATHE

Words and Music by HOLLY LAMAR
and STEPHANIE BENTLEY

Moderately fast

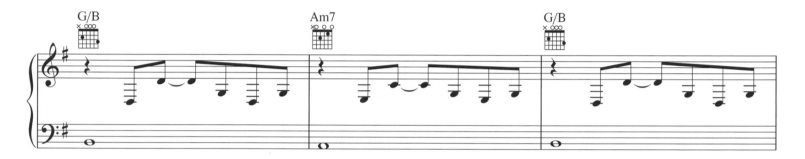

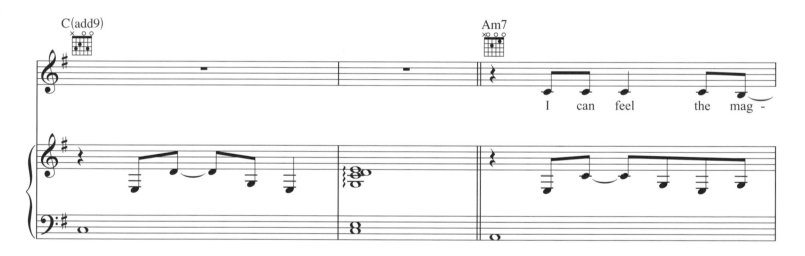

I can feel the mag -

- ic float - ing in _____ the air. _____

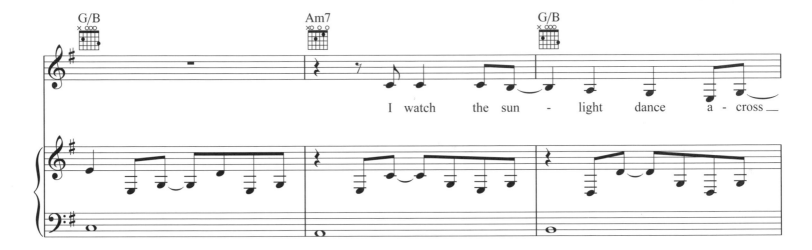

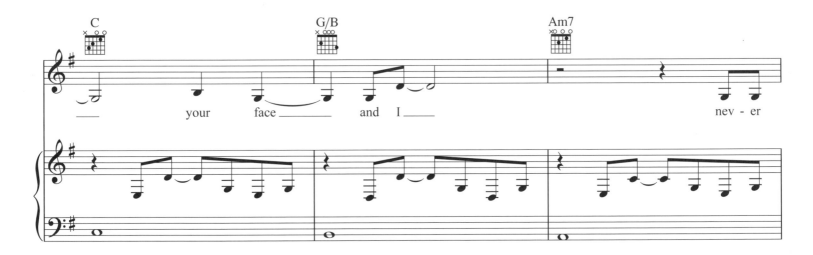

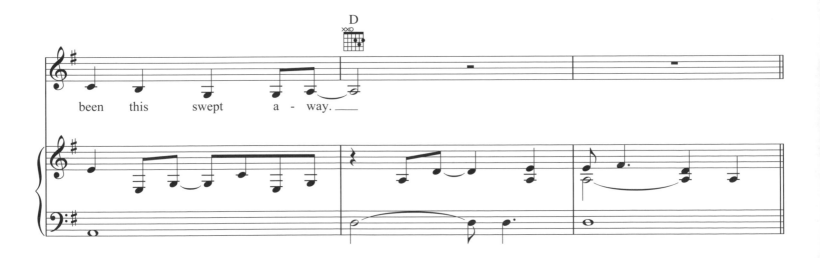

hear / is the beat-ing of ___ your heart. ___
know / there's no need for words ___ right now. ___

'Cause I can feel you breathe, it's wash-ing o - ver me, and sud-den - ly I'm

melt - ing in - to you. ___ There's noth-ing left to prove, ba - by, all we

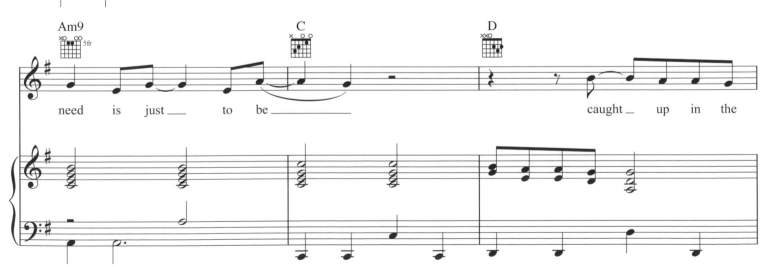

need is just ___ to be ___ caught ___ up in the

touch, the slow and stead-y rush. Ba-by, is-n't that the way ___ that love's ___

___ sup-posed ___ to be?

To Coda ⊕

I can feel you breathe. ___

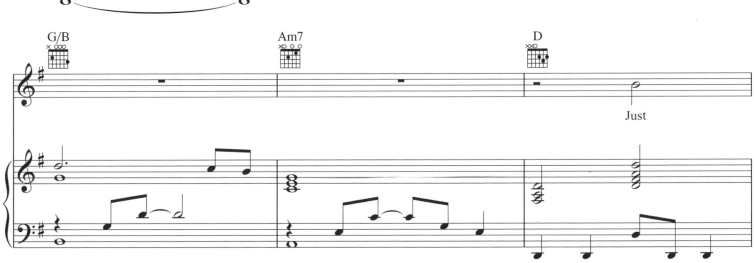

Just

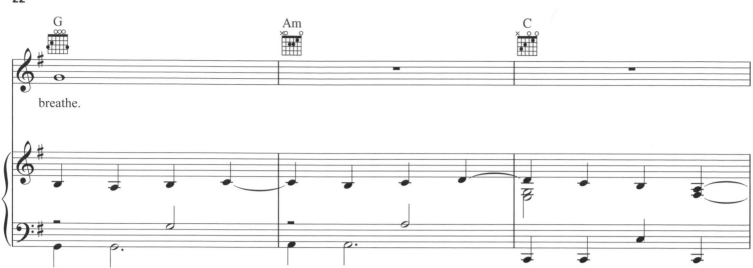

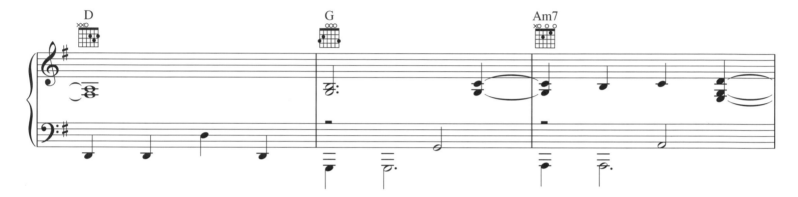

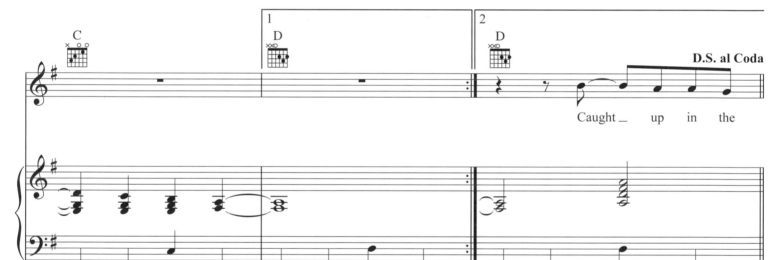

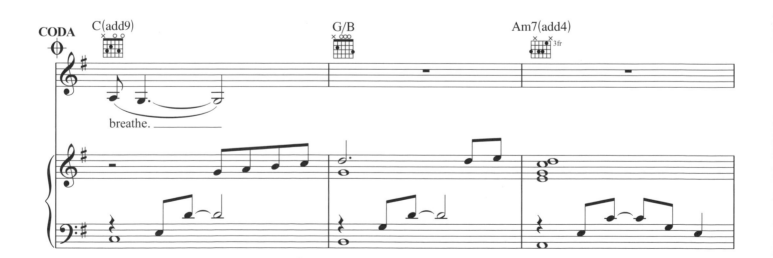

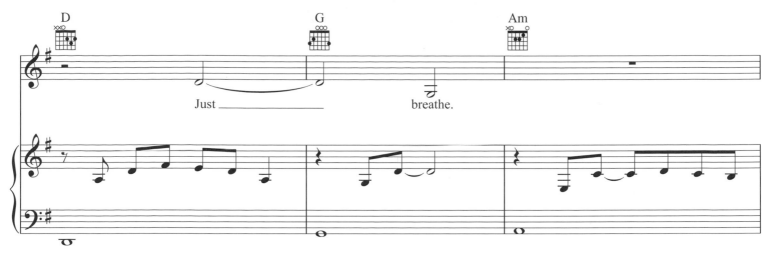

Just _____ breathe.

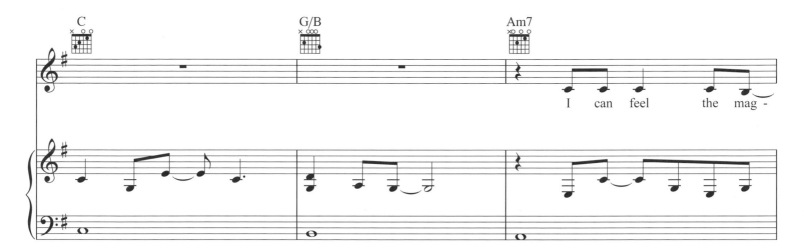

I can feel _____ the mag -

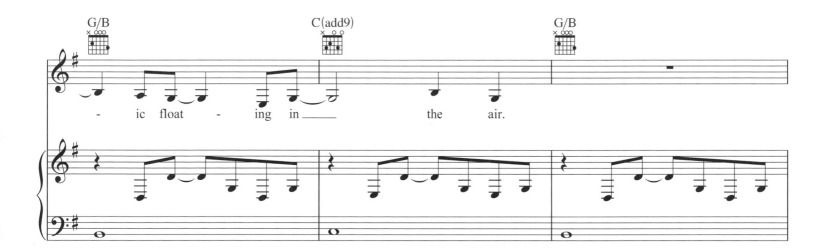

- ic float - ing in _____ the air.

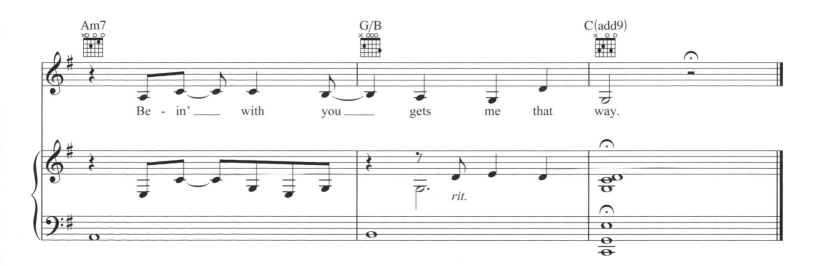

Be - in' _____ with you _____ gets me that way.

BEAUTIFUL

Words and Music by
LINDA PERRY

BECAUSE OF YOU

Words and Music by KELLY CLARKSON,
DAVID HODGES and BEN MOODY

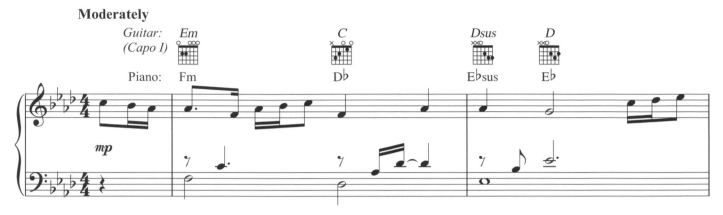

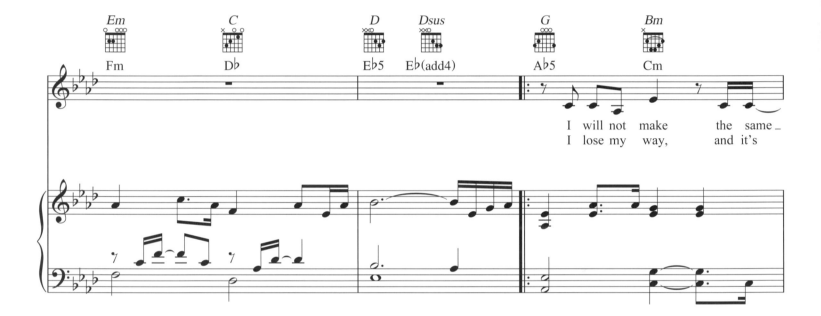

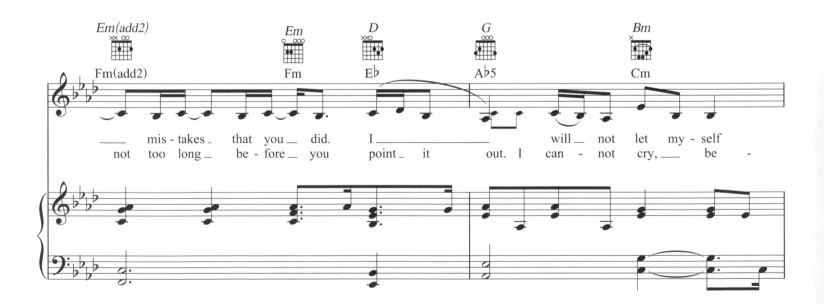

you I learned to play on the safe side, so I don't __ get hurt. __ Be-cause of

you I find it hard to trust not on-ly me, __ but ev-'ry-one a-round __ me. Be-cause of you, __

I am a-fraid. ____

I watched you die; I heard you cry ev-'ry night in your __

CHASING CARS

Words and Music by GARY LIGHTBODY,
TOM SIMPSON, PAUL WILSON,
JONATHAN QUINN and NATHAN CONNOLLY

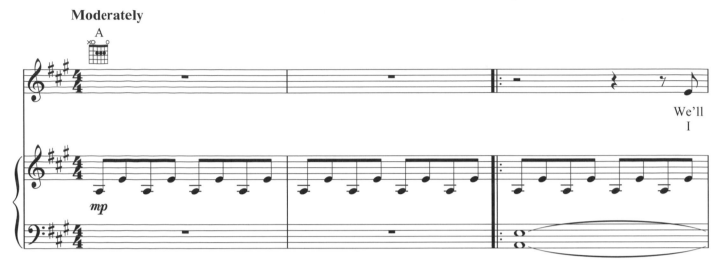

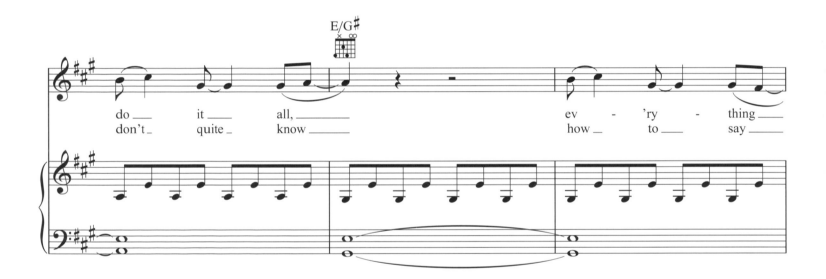

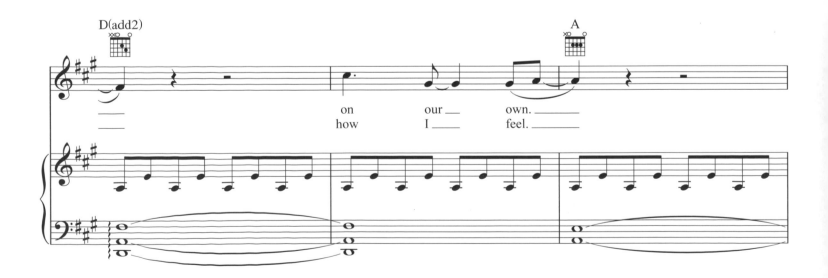

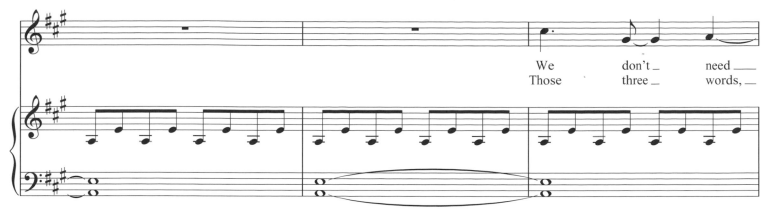

We don't _ need _____
Those three _ words, _

_____ an - y - thing _____ or
_____ I said _ too _ much, _____ then

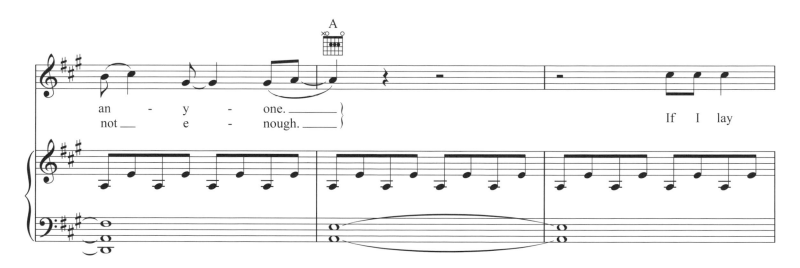

an - y - one. _____
not _ e - nough. _____

If I lay

here,
if I just lay here, _

Dmaj9

would you lie with me ___ and just for - get the world?

A

A

For - get what we're told ___ be - fore we get

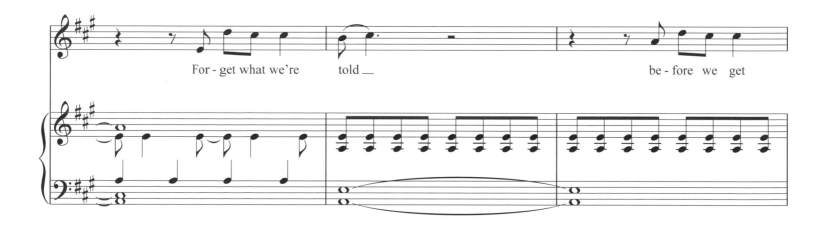

E(add4)/G#

D(add2)

too old. ___ Show me a gar - den ___ that's

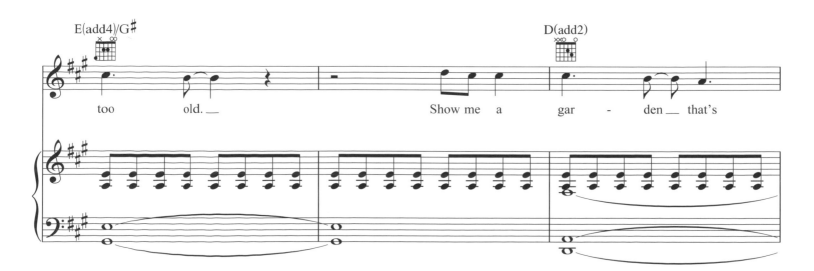

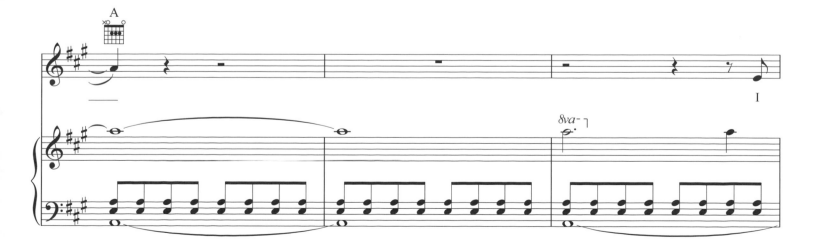

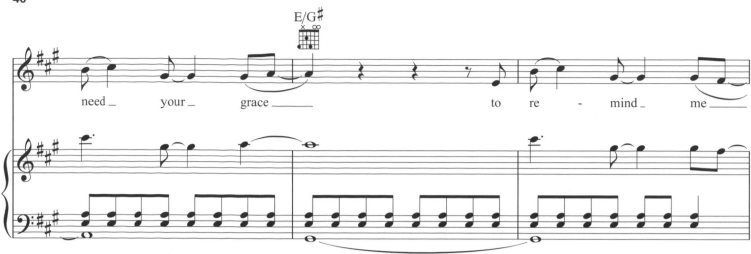

need your grace to re - mind me

to find my own.

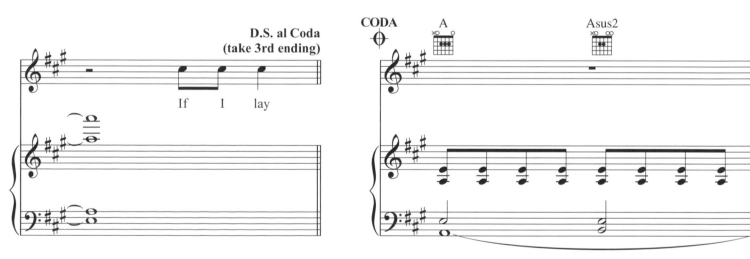

D.S. al Coda
(take 3rd ending)

If I lay

CODA

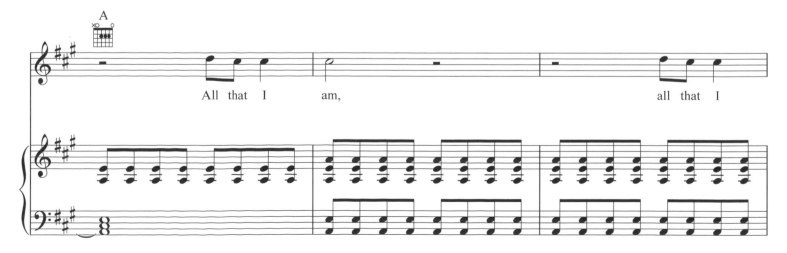

All that I am, all that I

ev - er was __ is here in your per - fect __ eyes,

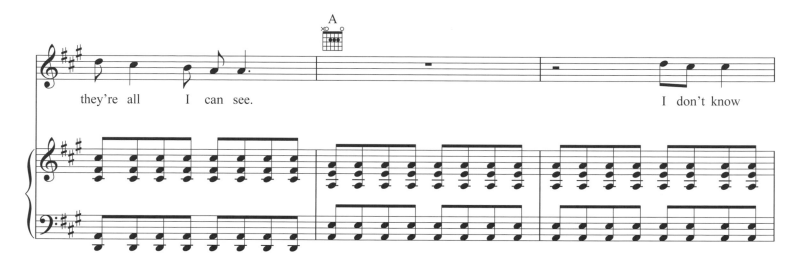

they're all I can see. I don't know

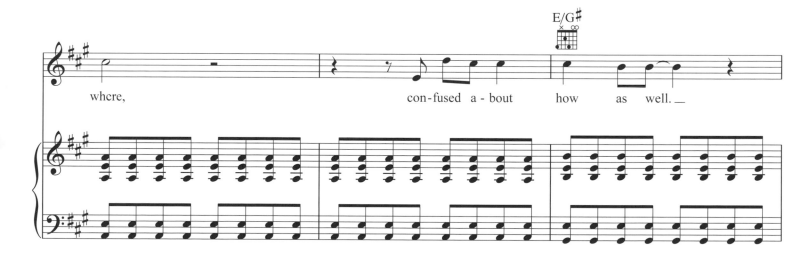

where, con-fused a-bout how as well. __

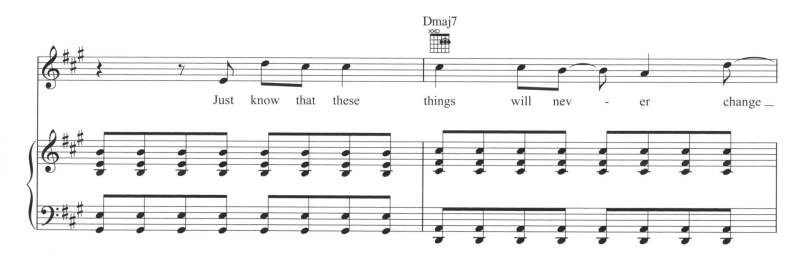

Just know that these things will nev - er change __

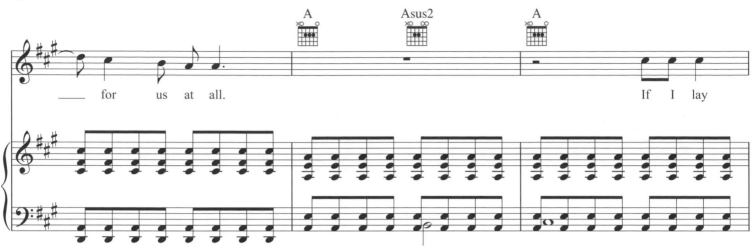

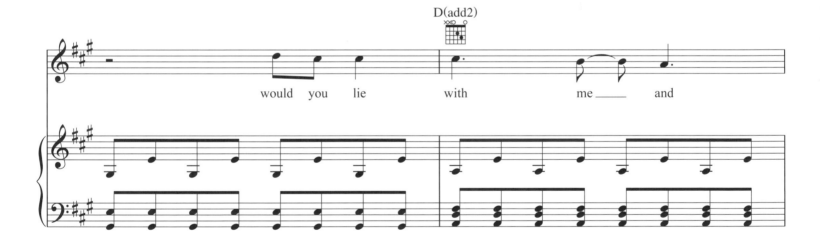

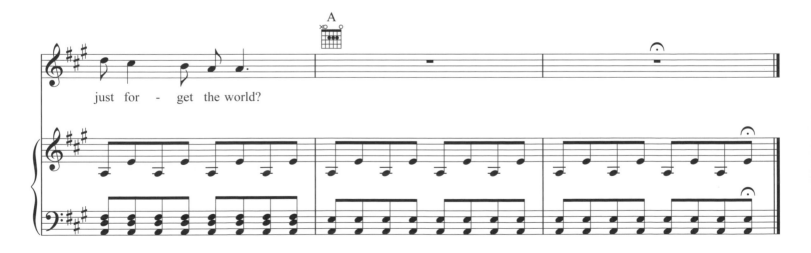

CLOCKS

Words and Music by GUY BERRYMAN,
JON BUCKLAND, WILL CHAMPION
and CHRIS MARTIN

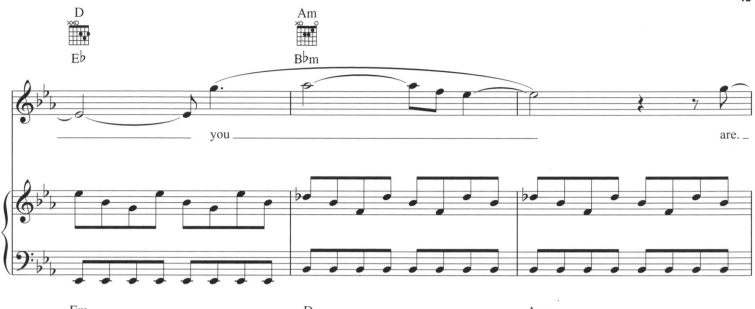

you _____ are. __

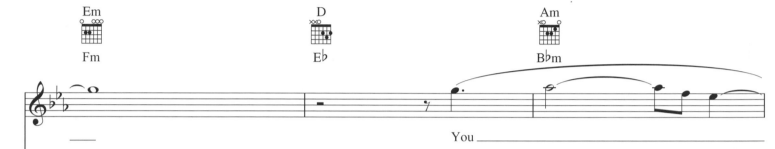

You _____

___ are. _____

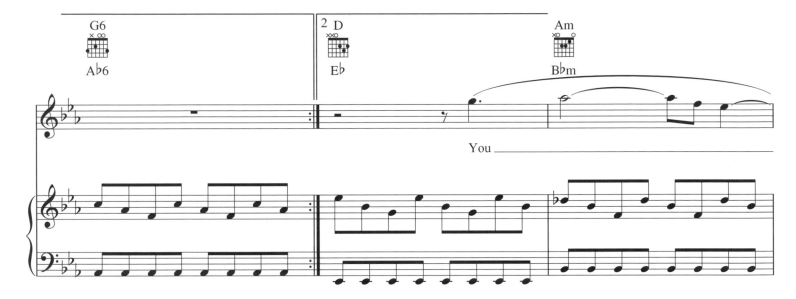

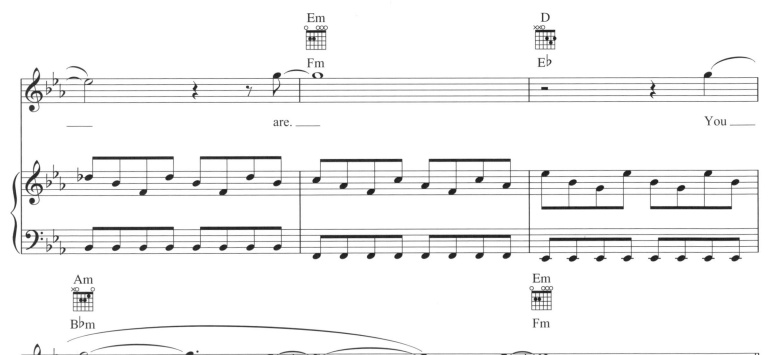

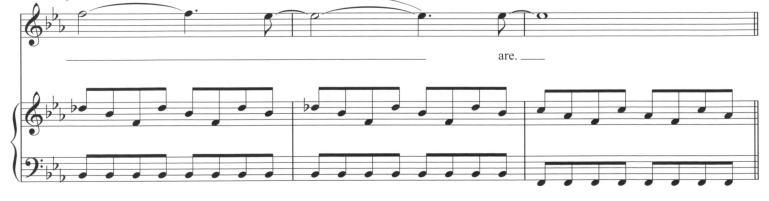

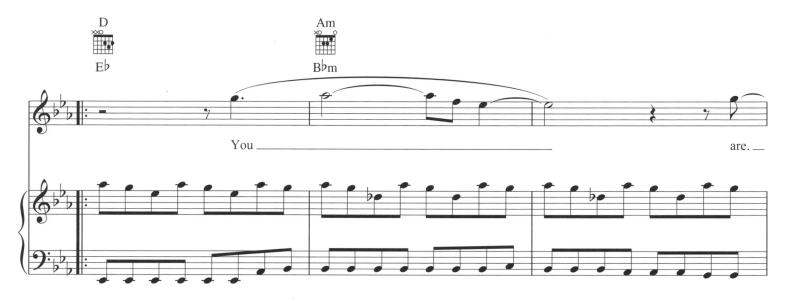

You _____ are. ___

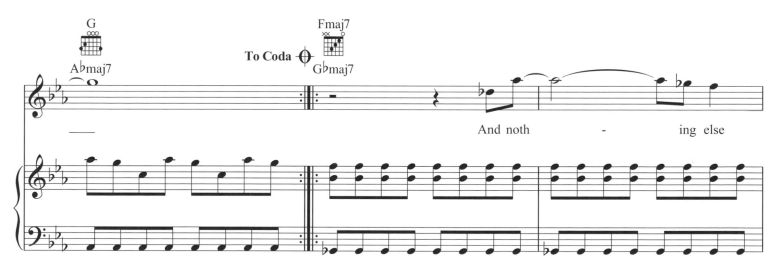

___ And noth - ing else

com - pares. _____

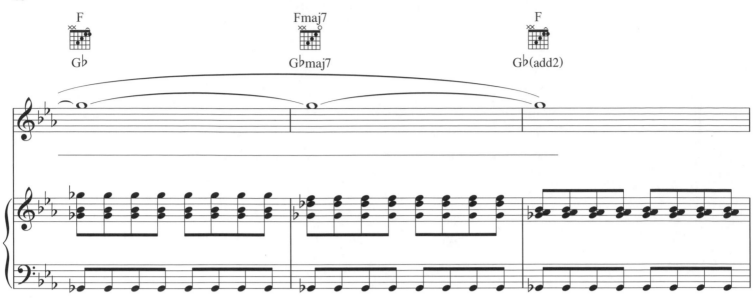

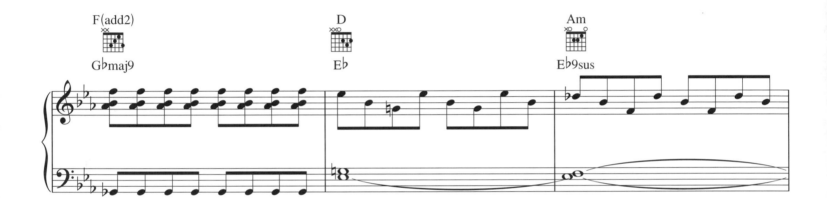

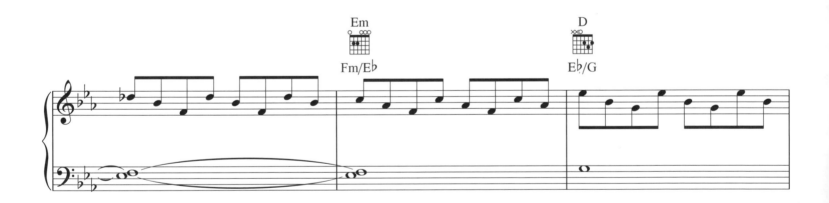

Home, home, _ where I want - ed _ to

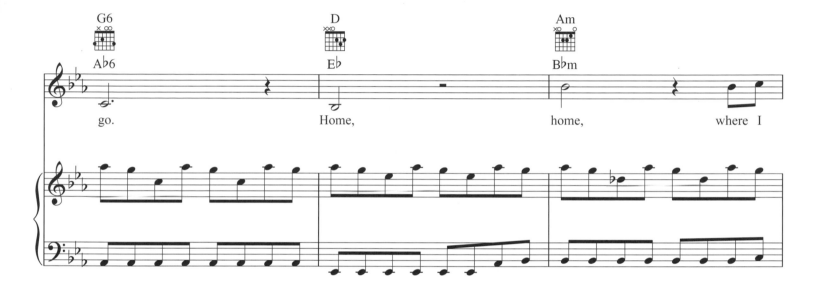

go. Home, home, where I

want - ed _ to go.

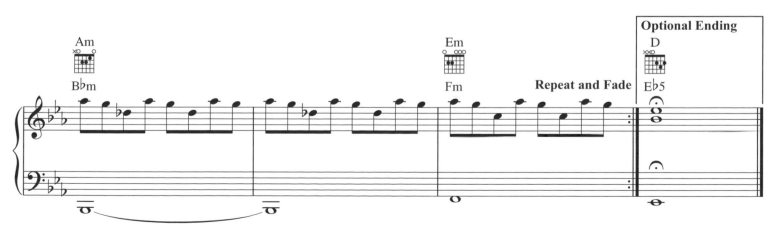

DROPS OF JUPITER
(Tell Me)

Words and Music by PAT MONAHAN,
JAMES STAFFORD, ROBERT HOTCHKISS,
CHARLES COLIN and SCOTT UNDERWOOD

Now that _____ she's back _____ in the at -
_____ she's back _____ from that soul

- mos - phere _____ with drops _____ of Ju - pi - ter in _____ her hair, _____ hey
_____ va - ca - tion, trac - ing her way _____ through the con - stel - la - tion,

hey, _____
hey _____ hey, _____

she acts ___ like sum - mer and walks ___ like rain, ___ re - minds ___
she checks ___ out Mo - zart while she does Tae - Bo, ___ re - minds ___

___ me that ___ there's a time to change, _ hey hey.
___ me that ___ there's ___ room to grow, ___ hey hey. _____

Since _
Now that _

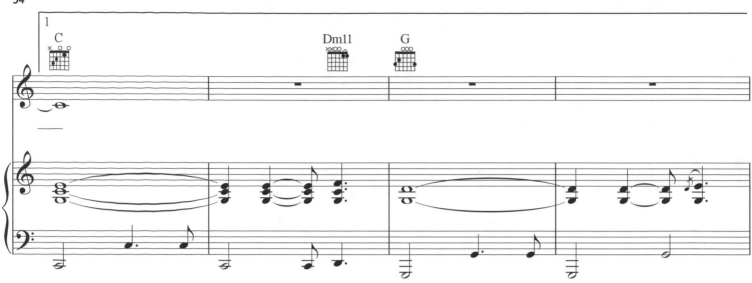

Now that ___

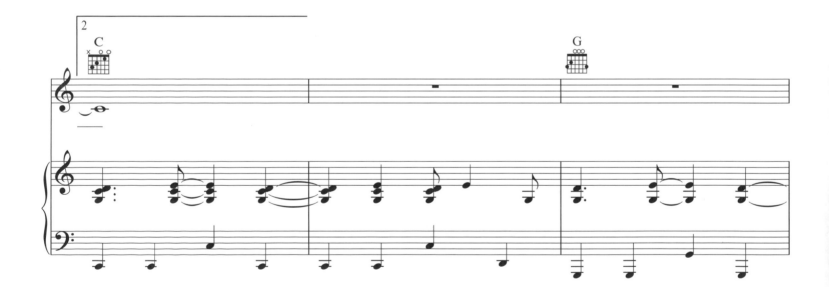

Can you i-mag-ine no love, pride,_ deep-fried chick-en, your

best friend _ al-ways stick-ing up for you,_____

___ e-ven when I know you're wrong?_ Can you i-mag-ine no

first dance,_ freeze-dried ro-mance, five-hour _ phone

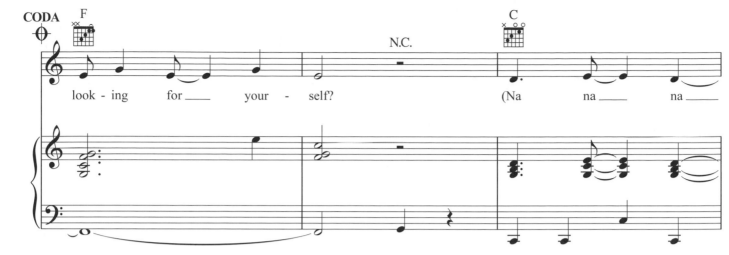

CODA

look - ing for ____ your - self? (Na na ____ na ____

___ na na na na na ____ na ____ na na na

na na na na.) ___ And did you fi - n'lly get the chance to dance __ a - long __ the light

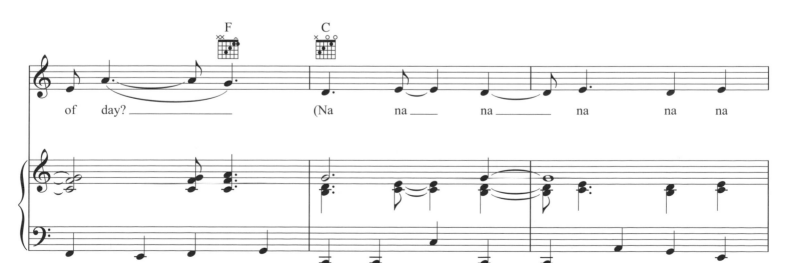

of day? _____ (Na na ____ na ____ na na na

JUST GIVE ME A REASON

Words and Music by ALECIA MOORE,
JEFF BHASKER and NATE RUESS

HELLO

Words and Music by ADELE ADKINS
and GREG KURSTIN

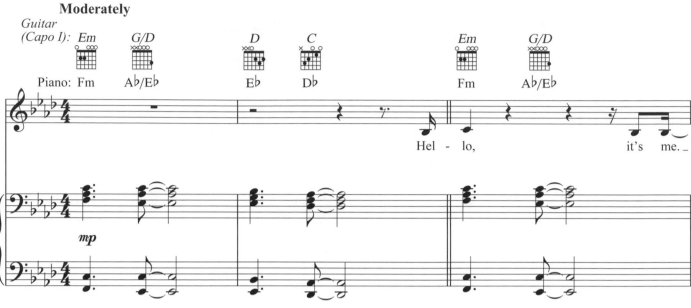

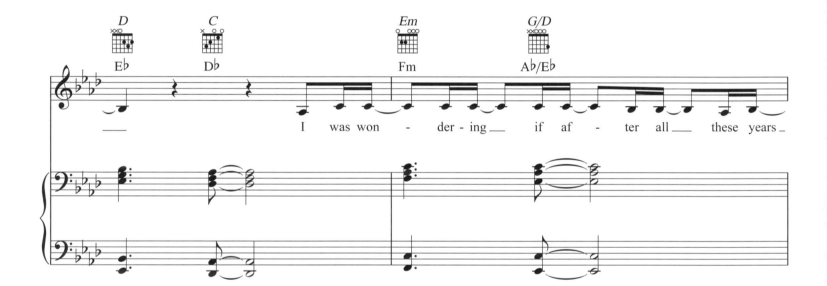

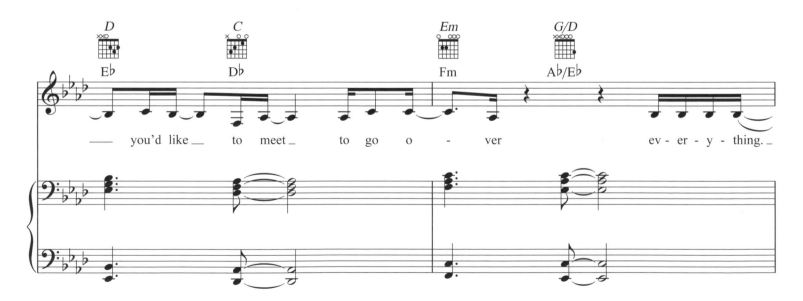

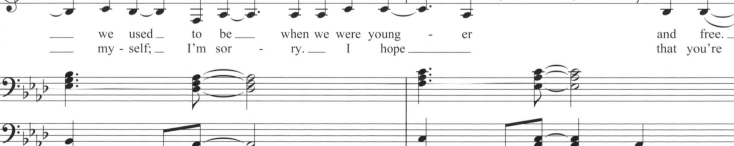

must have called a thou-sand times ___ to tell you ___ I'm sor-ry for ev-'ry-thing that I've done, ___ but when I call ___ you nev-er seem to be home. ___ Hel-lo from the out-side. ___ At

IF I AIN'T GOT YOU

Words and Music by
ALICIA KEYS

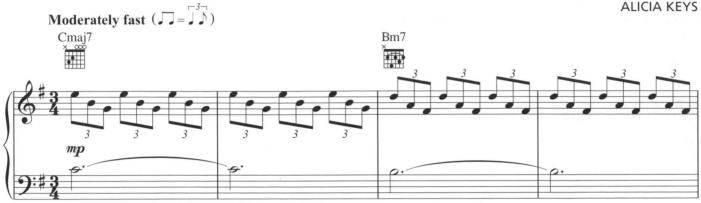

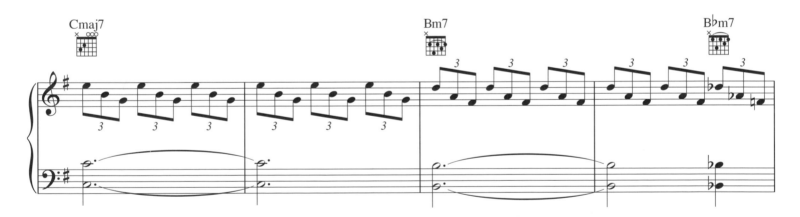

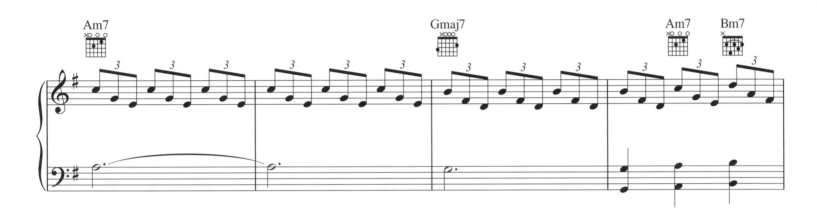

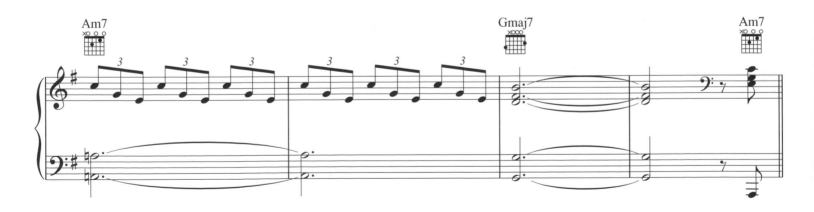

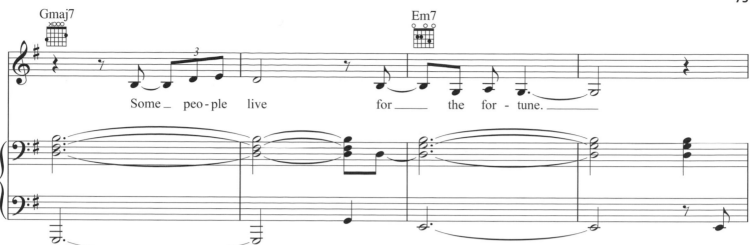

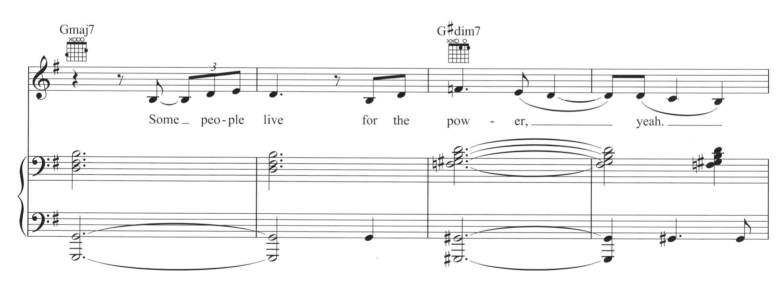

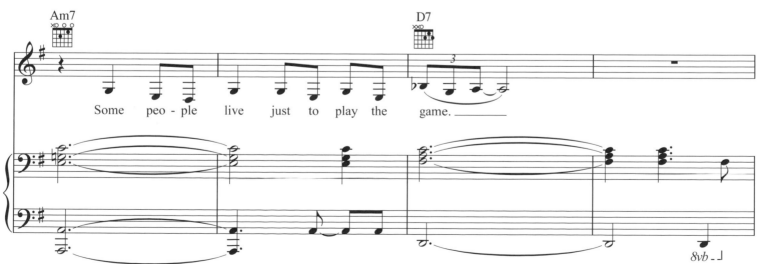

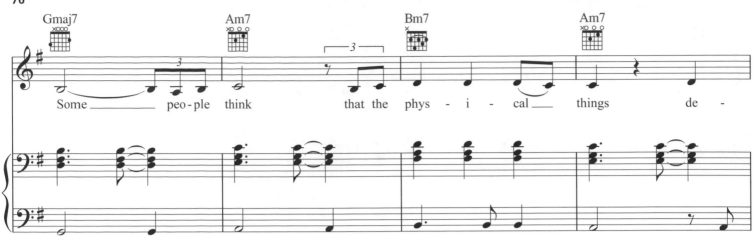

Some ____ peo-ple think that the phys - i - cal ____ things de -

fine ____ what's with - in. ____ And I've

been there be - fore, but that life's a ____ bore, so ____

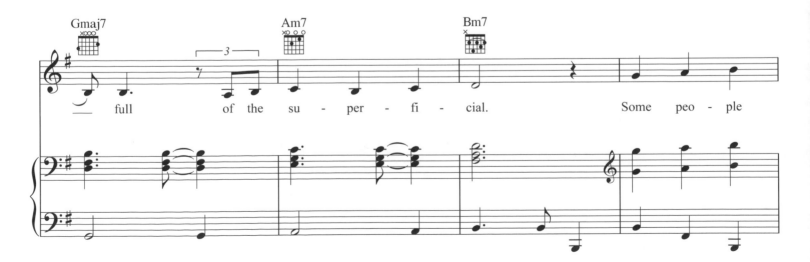

____ full of the su - per - fi - cial. Some peo - ple

sil - ver plat - ter, and ___ what good ___ would it

be ___ with no ___ one to share, with no one who ___

D.S. al Coda

tru - ly cares ___ for ___ me? Some peo - ple

Straight 8ths

CODA

As before

you, ___ you, ___ you. ___ Some peo - ple want it all, ___ but

IF I WERE A BOY

Words and Music by TOBY GAD
and BRITTANY CARLSON

LIKE I'M GONNA LOSE YOU

Words and Music by CAITLYN ELIZABETH SMITH,
JUSTIN WEAVER and MEGHAN TRAINOR

Moderately, in 4

Female: I found my-self dream - ing ___ in sil - ver and gold, ___ like a scene from a mov - ie that ev - 'ry bro - ken heart ___ knows. We were walk - ing on moon - light, ___

lose you. _____ I'm gon - na hold you like I'm say - ing good -

bye. _____ Wher - ev - er we're stand - ing, _____ I won't take you for

grant - ed, _____ 'cause we'll nev - er know when, when we'll run out of

time. _____ So, I'm gon - na love you like I'm gon - na

like I'm gon - na lose you.

lose you.

Love, ooh, like I'm gon - na

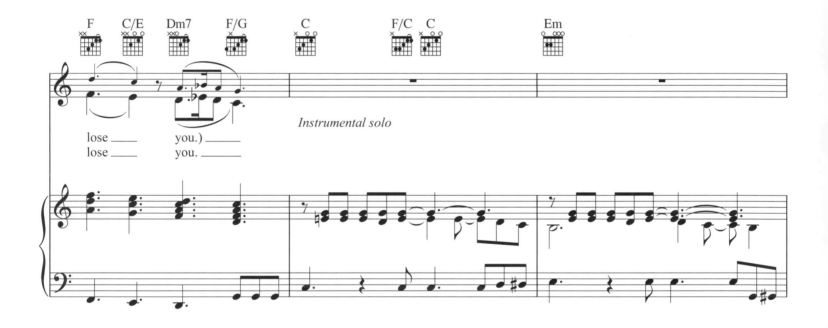

lose you.) lose you.

Instrumental solo

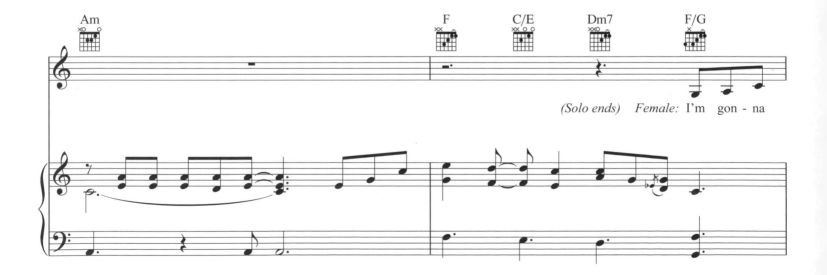

(Solo ends) *Female:* I'm gon - na

Male: (Oh, ___ like I'm gon - na lose you.

love you ___ like I'm gon - na lose you. I'm gon - na

D.S. al Coda

hold you... ___ ...bye.) ___ (Both): Wher-ev - er we're
hold you like I'm say-ing good - bye. ___

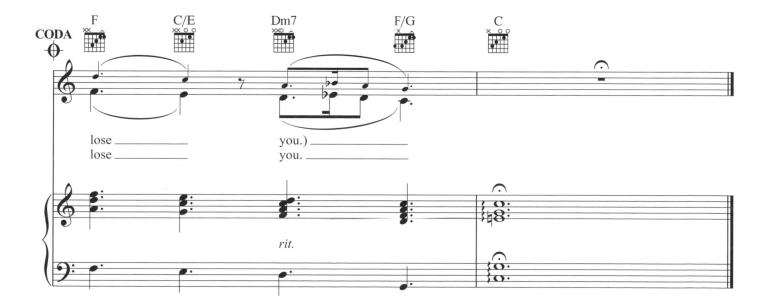

lose ___ you.) ___
lose ___ you.

rit.

LOOK WHAT YOU MADE ME DO

Words and Music by TAYLOR SWIFT,
JACK ANTONOFF, RICHARD FAIRBRASS,
FRED FAIRBRASS and ROB MANZOLI

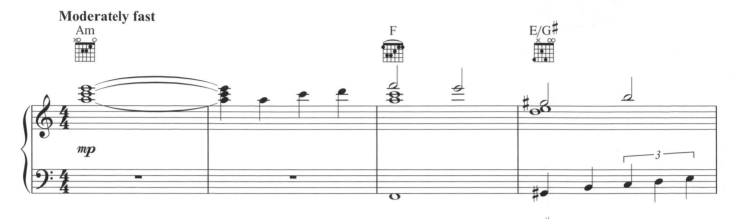

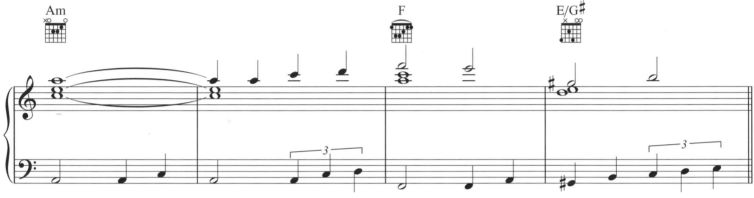

I don't like your lit-tle games, don't like your tilt-ed
I don't like your per-fect crime, how you laugh when you

stage. The role you made me play of the fool. No, I don't like you.
lie. You said the gun was mine. Is-n't cool. No, I

To Coda

do. Look what you just made me do, look what you just made me...

Ooh, look what you made me do, look what you made me do. Look what you just made

me do, look what you just made me do. I don't like your king - dom

keys, they once be - longed to me. You

MILLION REASONS

Words and Music by STEFANI GERMANOTTA,
MARK RONSON and HILLARY LINDSEY

LOST BOY

Words and Music by
RUTH BERHE

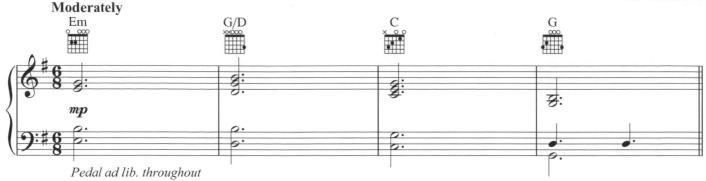

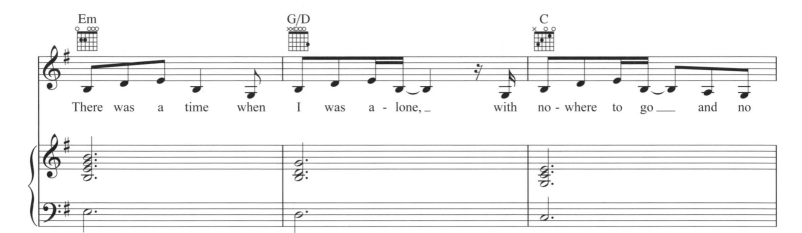

There was a time when I was a-lone, with no-where to go and no

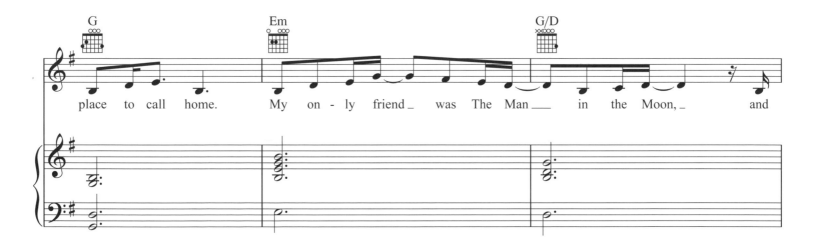

place to call home. My on-ly friend was The Man in the Moon, and

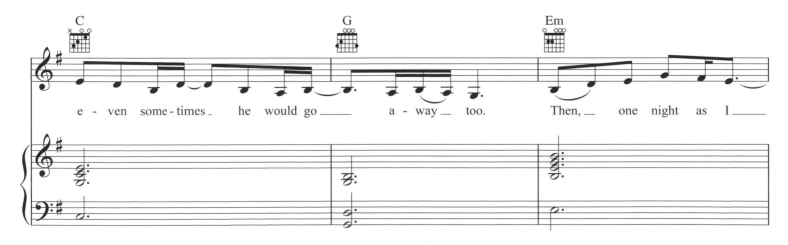

e-ven some-times he would go a-way too. Then, one night as I

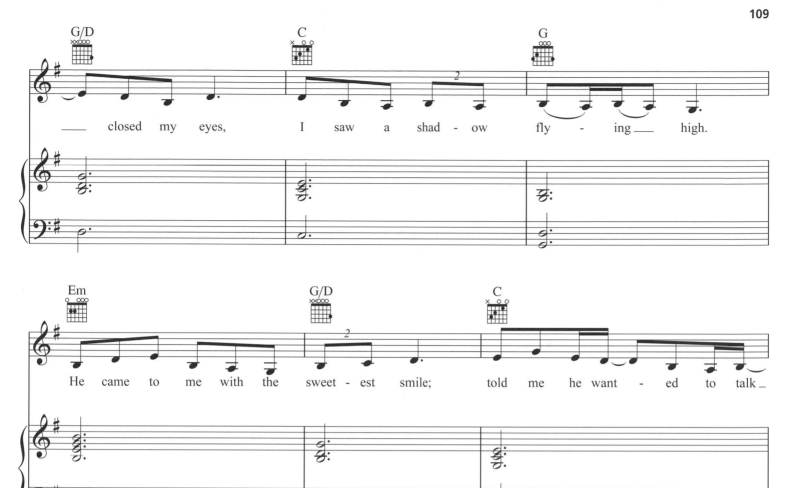

_____ closed my eyes, I saw a shad - ow fly - ing _____ high.

He came to me with the sweet - est smile; told me he want - ed to talk _____

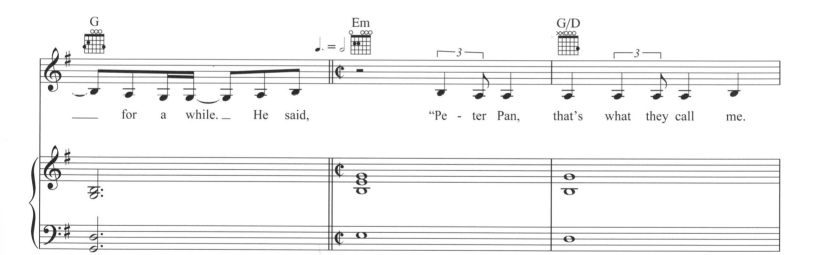

_____ for a while. _____ He said, "Pe - ter Pan, that's what they call me.

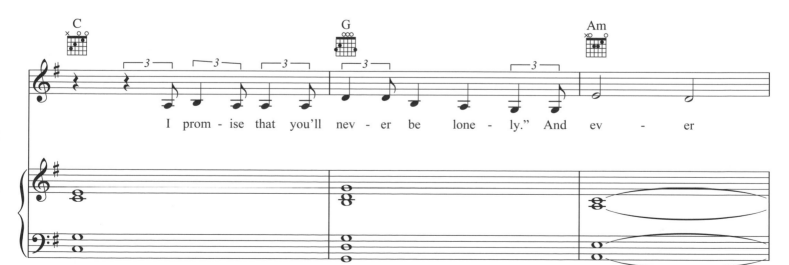

I prom - ise that you'll nev - er be lone - ly." And ev - er

since that ___ day... ___

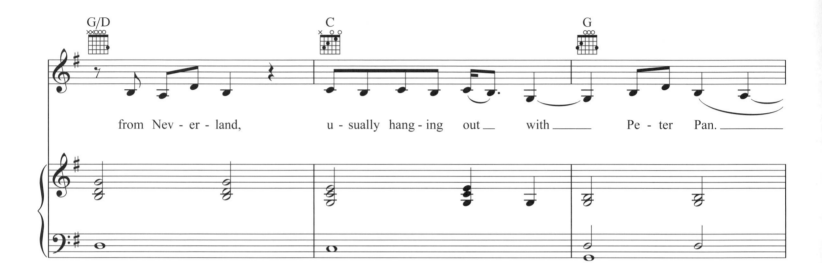

I am a lost boy from Nev - er - land, u - sually hang - ing out ___ with ___ Pe - ter Pan. ___

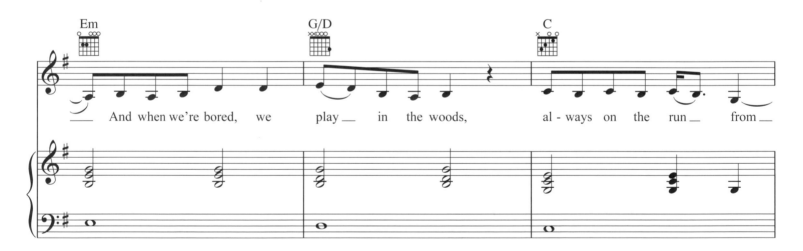

___ And when we're bored, we play ___ in the woods, al - ways on the run ___ from ___

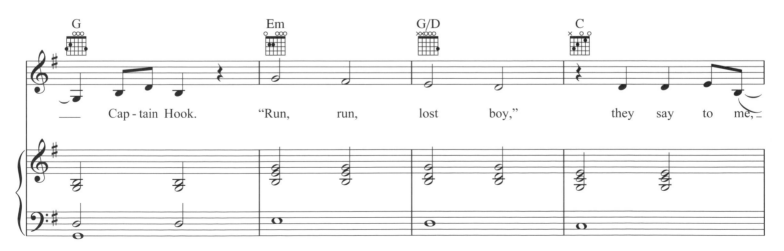

___ Cap - tain Hook. "Run, run, lost boy," they say to me, ___

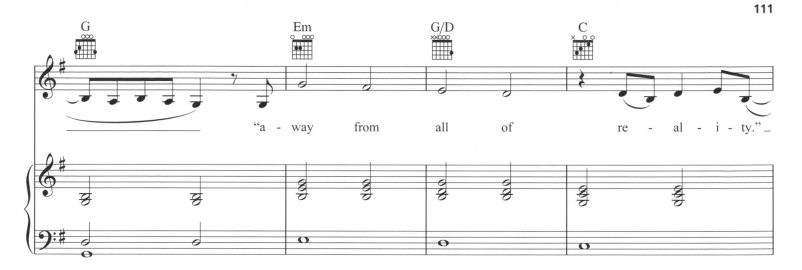

"a - way from all of re - al - i - ty."

Nev - er - land is home to the lost boys like me; and

lost boys like me are free. Nev - er - land is home to the lost boys like me; and

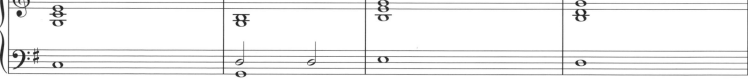

To Coda

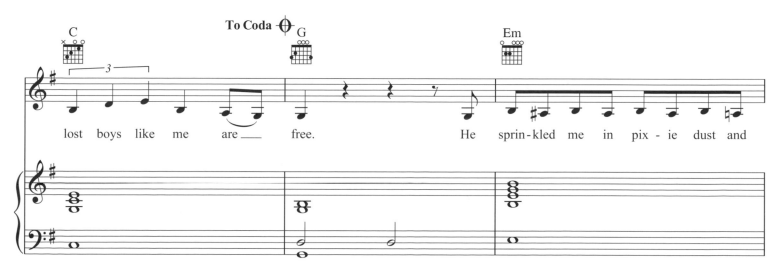

lost boys like me are free. He sprin - kled me in pix - ie dust and

told me to be-lieve, be-lieve in him and be-lieve in me. "To-

geth-er, we will fly a-way in a cloud of green, to your beau-ti-ful des-ti-ny." As we

soared a-bove the town that nev-er loved me, I re-al-ized I fi-n'lly had a

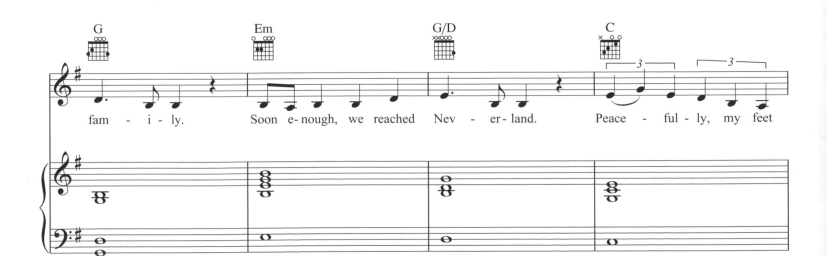

fam - i - ly. Soon e-nough, we reached Nev - er-land. Peace-ful-ly, my feet

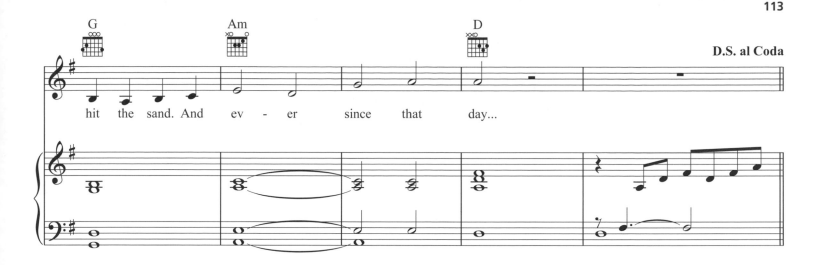

D.S. al Coda

hit the sand. And ev - er since that day...

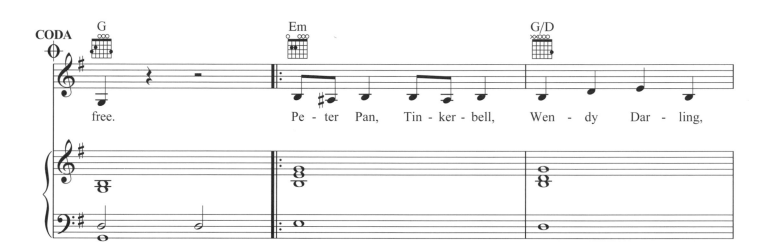

CODA

free.

Pe - ter Pan, Tin - ker - bell, Wen - dy Dar - ling,

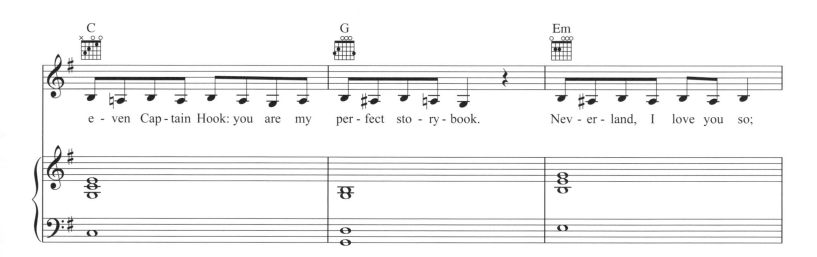

e - ven Cap - tain Hook: you are my per - fect sto - ry - book. Nev - er - land, I love you so;

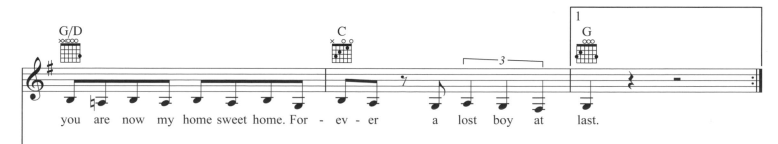

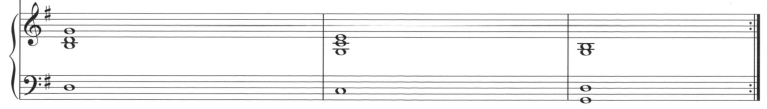

you are now my home sweet home. For - ev - er a lost boy at last.

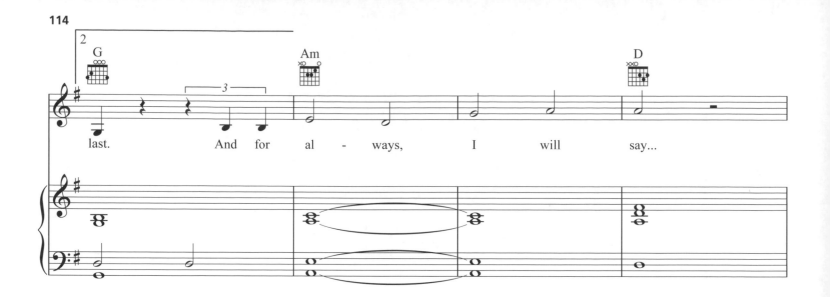

last. And for al - ways, I will say...

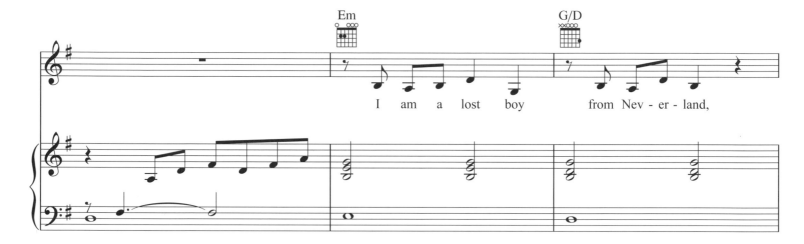

I am a lost boy from Nev - er - land,

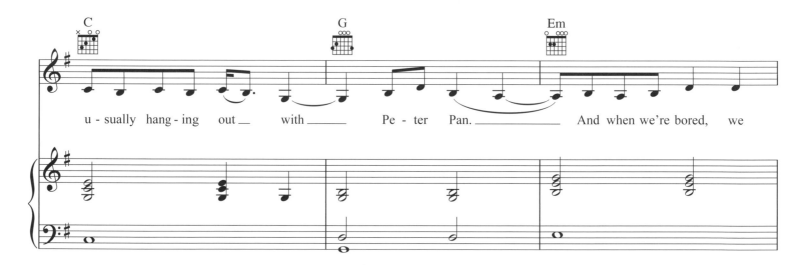

u - sually hang - ing out __ with ___ Pe - ter Pan. _____ And when we're bored, we

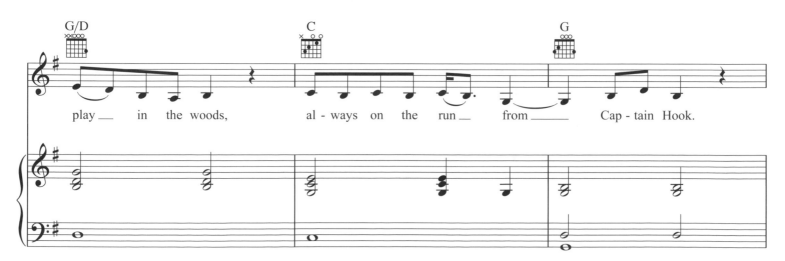

play __ in the woods, al - ways on the run __ from ___ Cap - tain Hook.

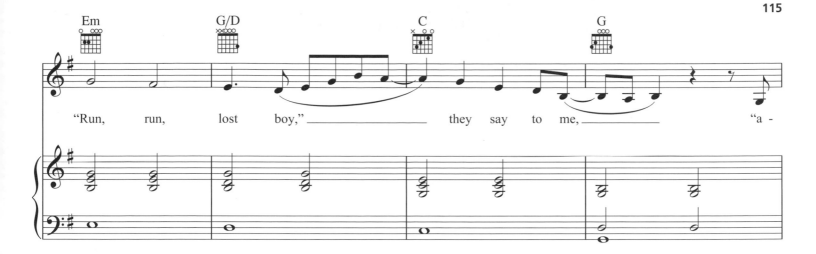

"Run, run, lost boy," they say to me, "a-

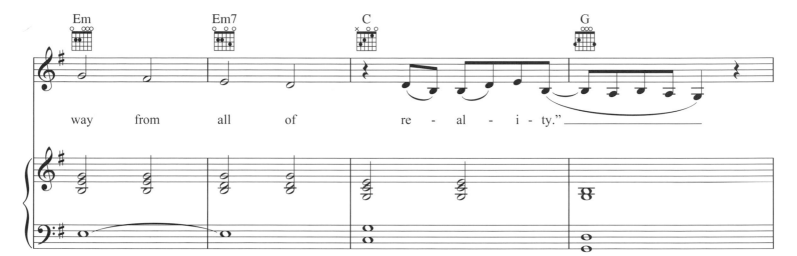

way from all of re - al - i - ty."

Nev - er - land is home to the lost boys like me; and lost boys like me are free.

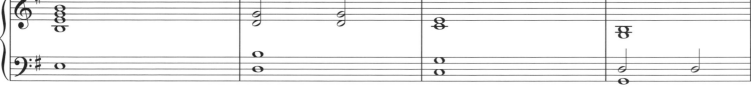

Nev - er - land is home to the lost boys like me; and lost boys like me are free.

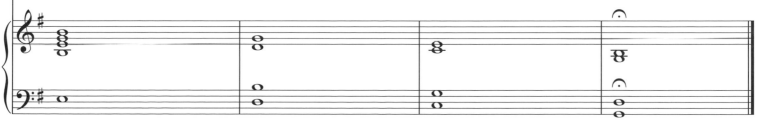

LOVE SONG

Words and Music by
SARA BAREILLES

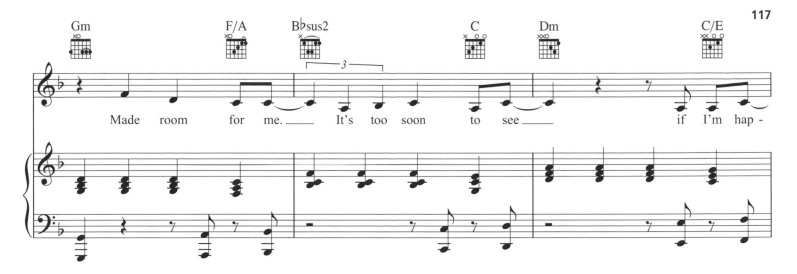

Made room for me. ___ It's too soon to see ___ if I'm hap -

- py in your hands. ___ I'm un - us - ual - ly ___ hard ___ to hold on ___

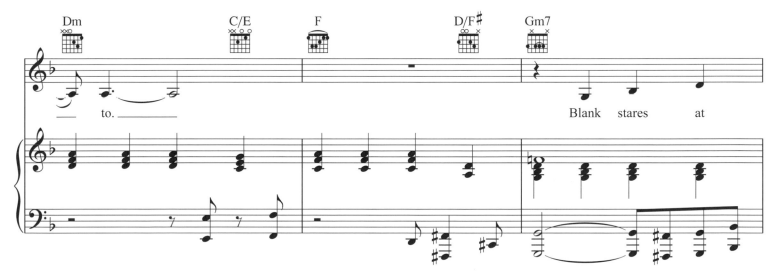

___ to. ___ Blank stares at

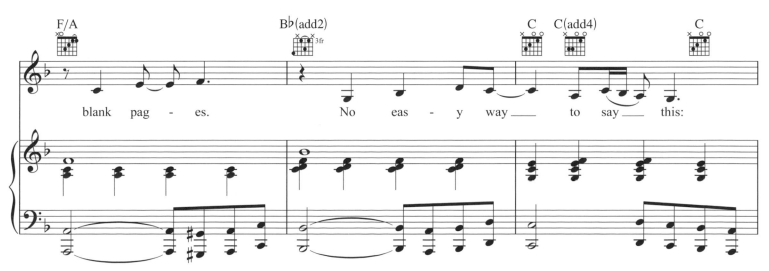

blank pag - es. No eas - y way ___ to say ___ this:

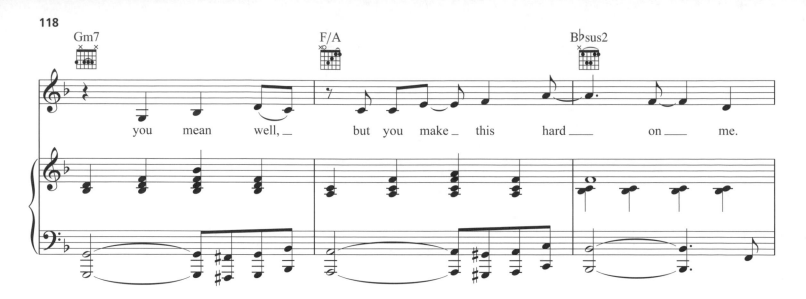

you mean well, __ but you make __ this hard __ on __ me.

I'm not gon-na write you __ a love song __ 'cause you ask __ for it, 'cause you need __

__ one. You see, __ I'm not gon - na write you __ a

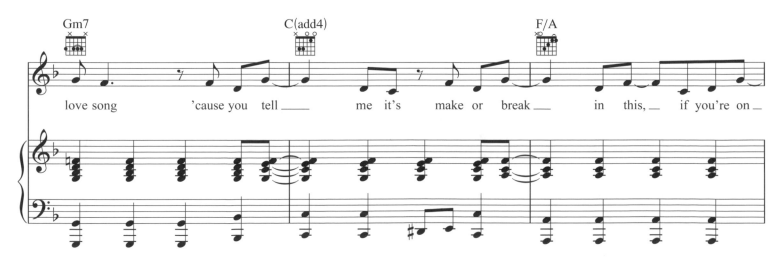

love song 'cause you tell __ me it's make or break __ in this, __ if you're on __

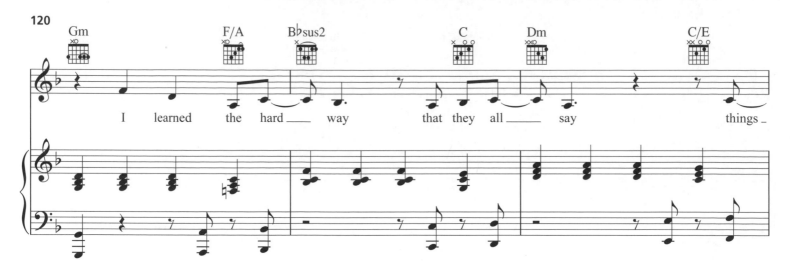

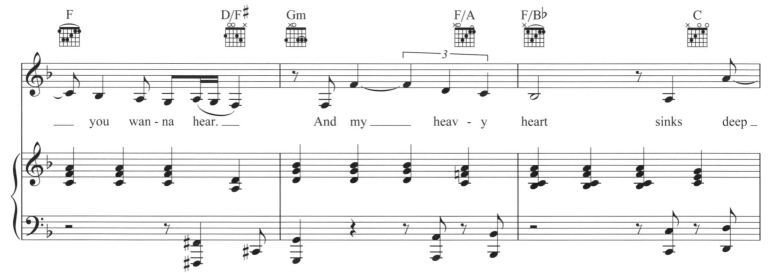

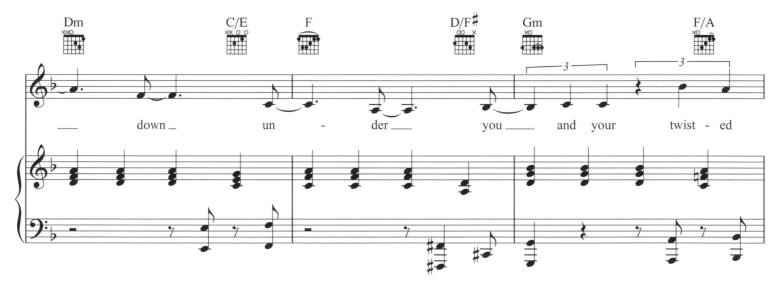

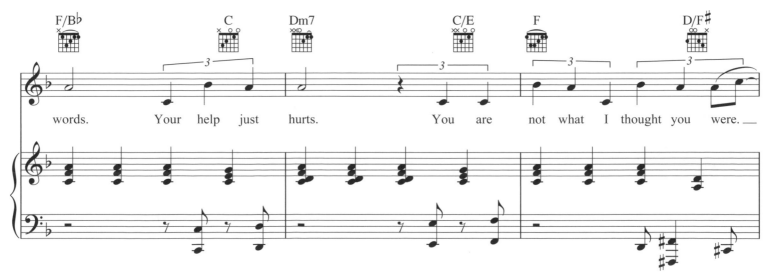

122

walk the sev-en seas when I be - lieve that there's a rea - son to write___ you a love___

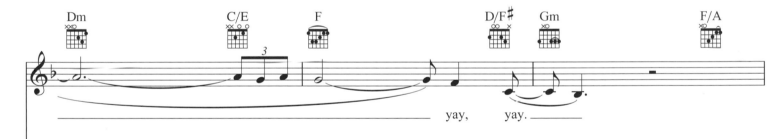

___ song to - day, ___ to - day, ___

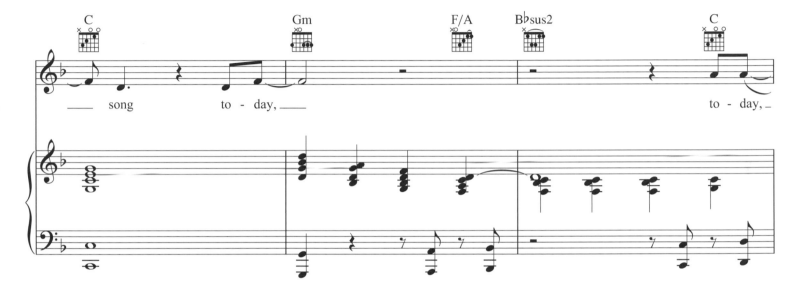

yay, yay. ___

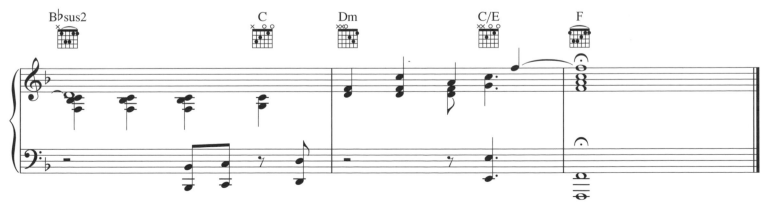

100 YEARS

Words and Music by
JOHN ONDRASIK

Moderately fast

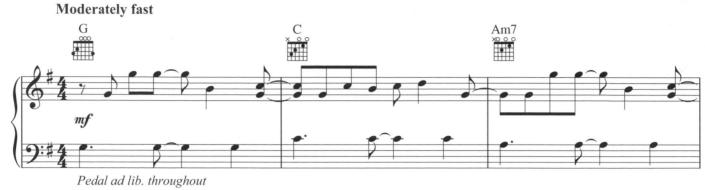

Pedal ad lib. throughout

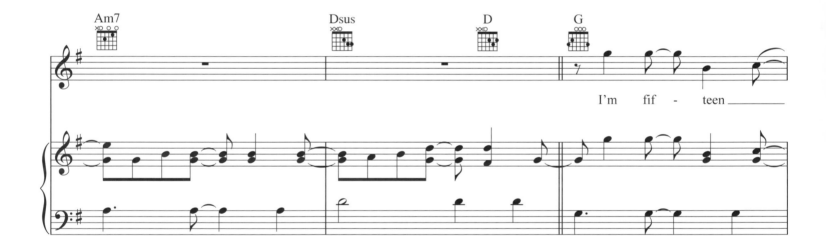

I'm fif - teen _____

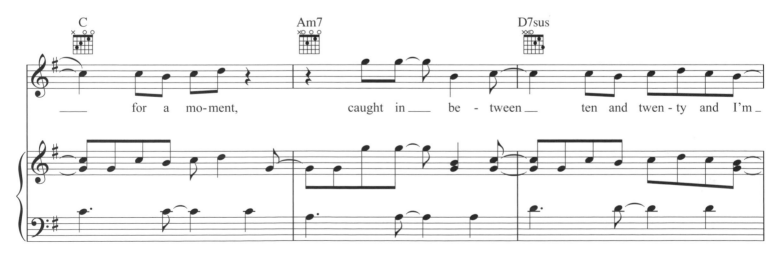

_____ for a mo - ment,   caught in _____ be - tween _____ ten and twen - ty and I'm _____

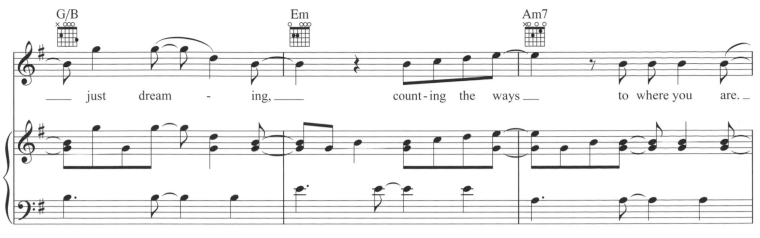

just dream - ing, ____ count-ing the ways ____ to where you are. ____

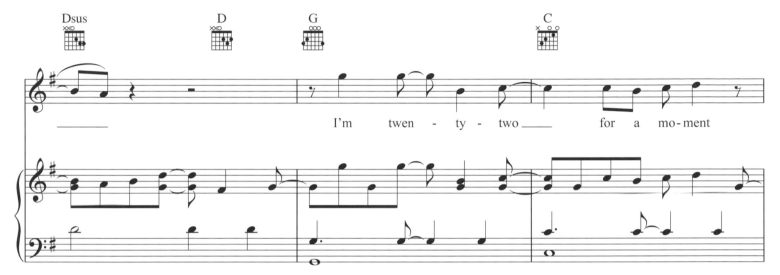

____ I'm twen - ty-two ____ for a mo - ment

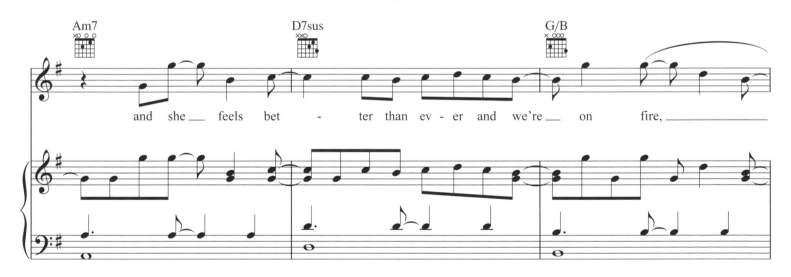

and she ___ feels bet - ter than ev - er and we're ___ on fire, _____

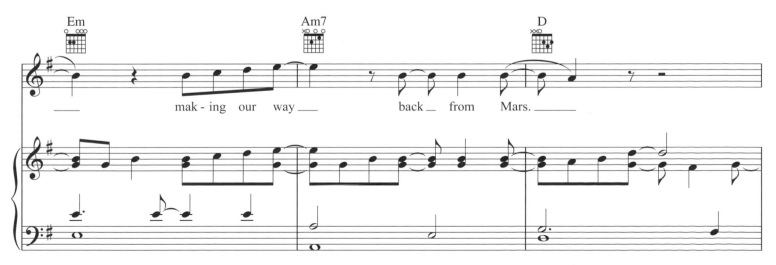

____ mak - ing our way ____ back ___ from Mars. _____

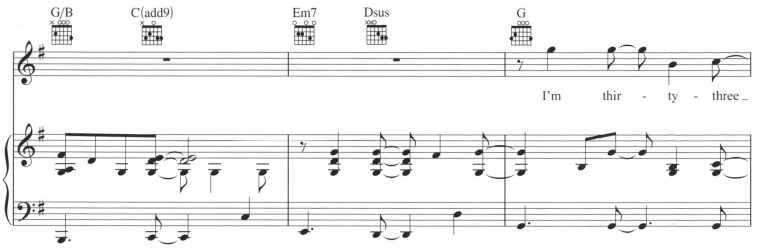

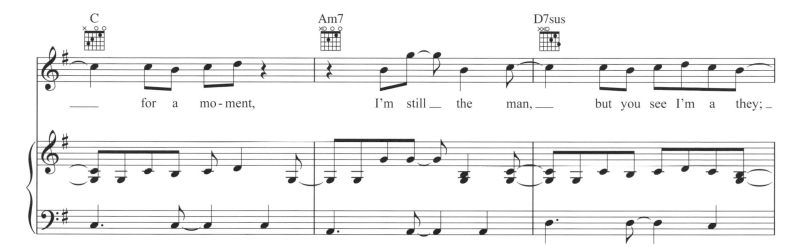

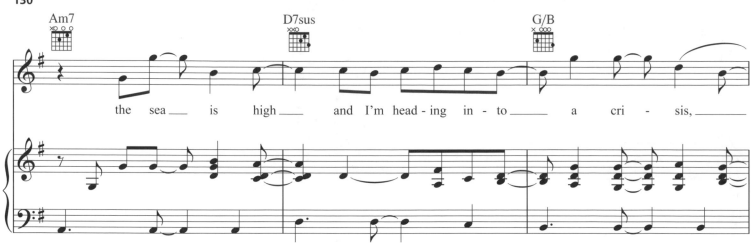

the sea __ is high __ and I'm head-ing in-to __ a cri - sis, __

__ chas-ing the years __ of __ my life. __

Fif - teen, there's __ still time __ for you. __ Time __ to buy __

__ and time __ to lose __ your - self __ with - in __ a morn - ing star. __

Fif - teen, I'm

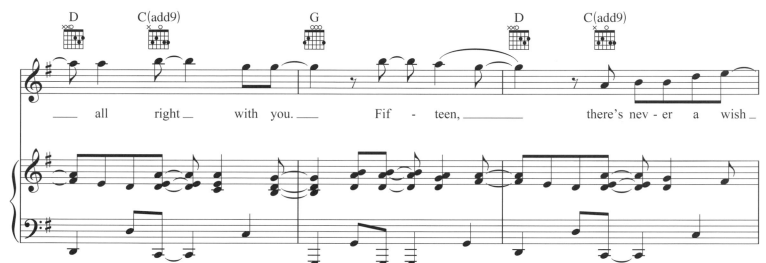

all right with you. Fif - teen, there's nev - er a wish

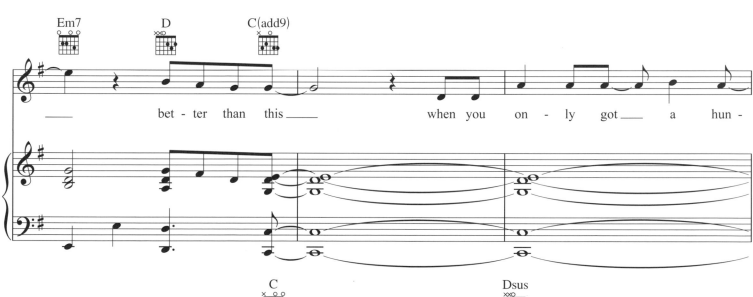

bet - ter than this when you on - ly got a hun -

- dred years to live. Half time goes by, sud - den - ly you're wise.

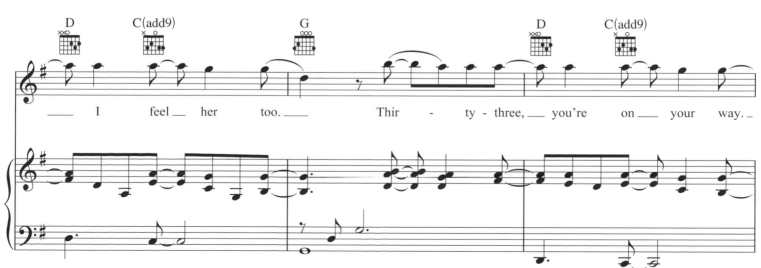

RISE UP

Words and Music by CASSANDRA BATIE
and JENNIFER DECILVEO

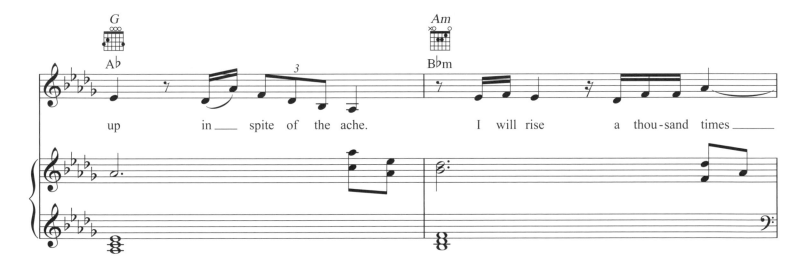

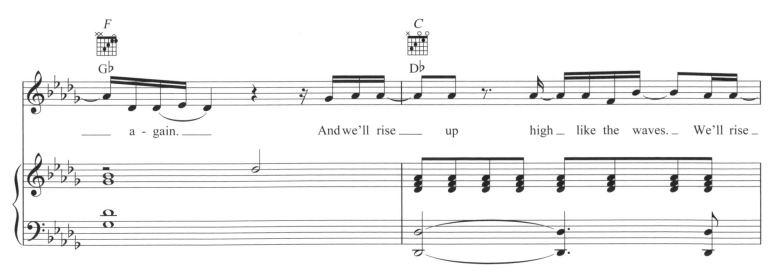

ROAR

Words and Music by KATY PERRY,
MAX MARTIN, DR. LUKE,
BONNIE McKEE and HENRY WALTER

I used to bite my tongue and hold __ my breath, scared to rock the boat and make __ a mess.

So I sat qui-et-ly, a - greed po-lite - ly.

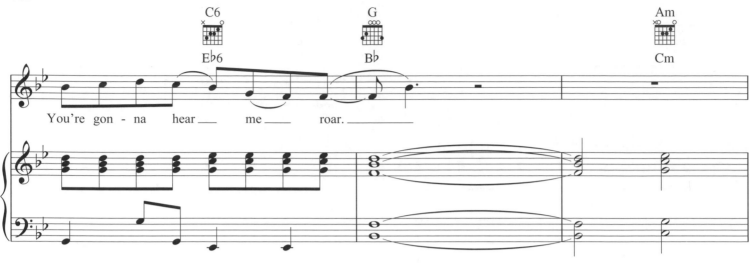

ROYALS

Words and Music by ELLA YELICH-O'CONNOR
and JOEL LITTLE

Moderately slow

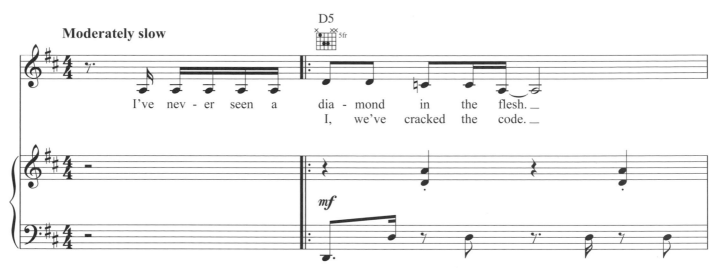

I've nev-er seen a dia-mond in the flesh.
I, we've cracked the code.

I cut my teeth on wed-ding rings in the
We count our dol-lars on the train to the

mov-ies. And I'm not proud of my ad-dress,
par-ty. And ev-'ry-one who knows us knows

You can call me Queen Bee. And ba-by, I'll rule; (I'll rule, I'll rule, I'll rule.)

let me live that fan-tas-y.

My friends and let me live that fan-tas-y.

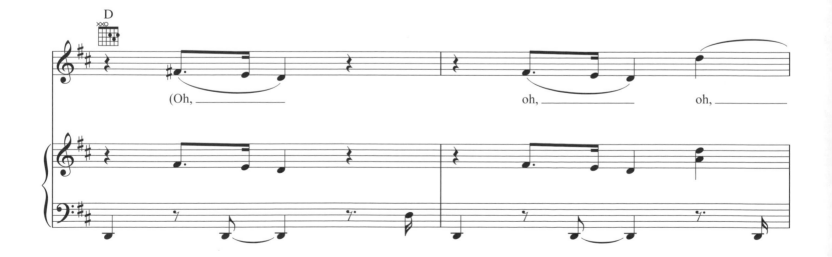

(Oh, oh, oh,

SAY SOMETHING

Words and Music by IAN AXEL,
CHAD VACCARINO and MIKE CAMPBELL

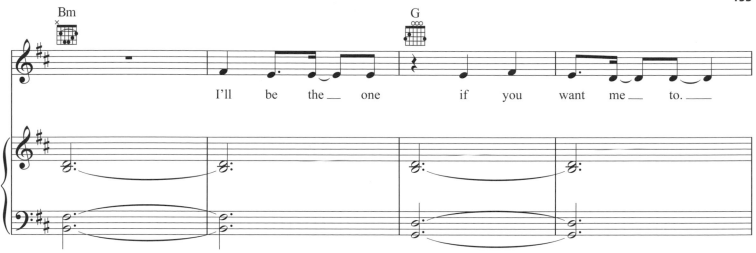

I'll be the ___ one if you want me ___ to. ___

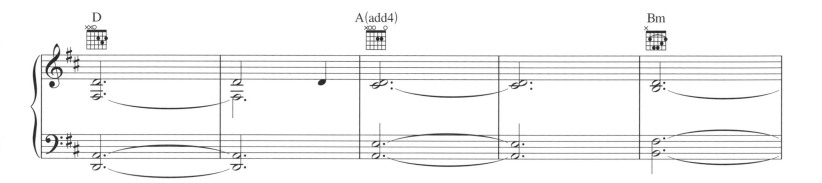

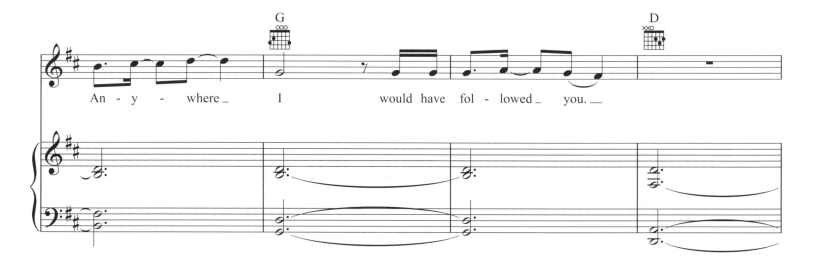

An - y - where ___ I would have fol - lowed ___ you. ___

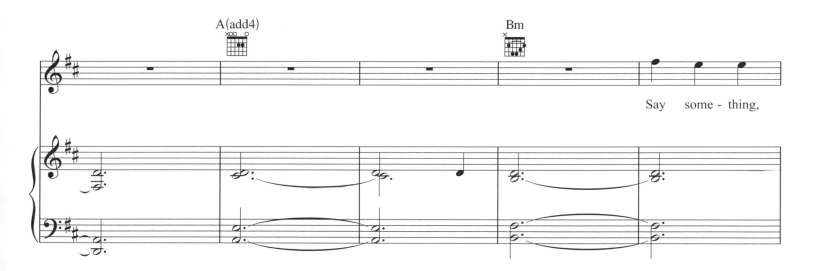

Say some - thing,

to you.
to you.

An - y - where _ }
And an - y - where _ }
I
would have fol - lowed _ you. _

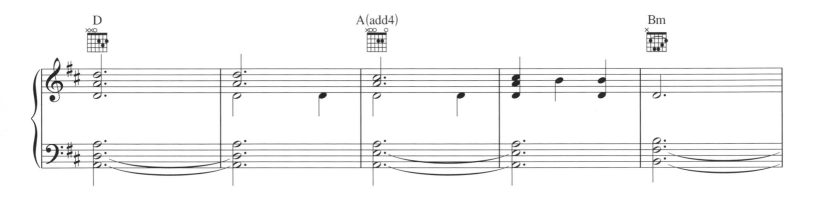

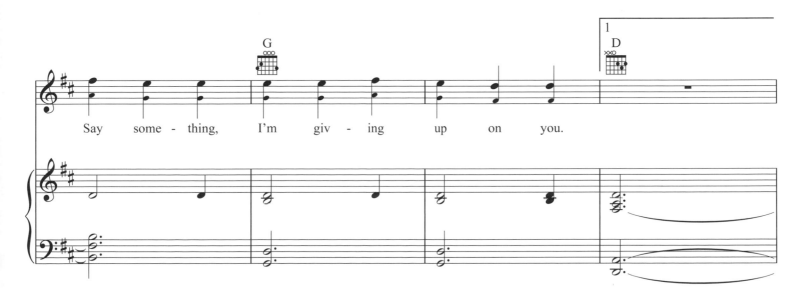

Say some - thing, I'm giv - ing up on you.

SAY YOU WON'T LET GO

Words and Music by STEVEN SOLOMON,
JAMES ARTHUR and NEIL ORMANDY

7 YEARS

Words and Music by LUKAS FORCHHAMMER,
MORTEN RISTORP, STEFAN FORREST,
DAVID LABREL, CHRISTOPHER BROWN
and MORTEN PILEGAARD

Moderately slow, in 2

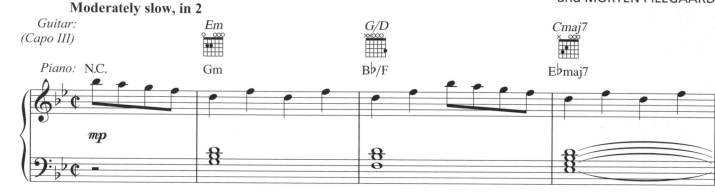

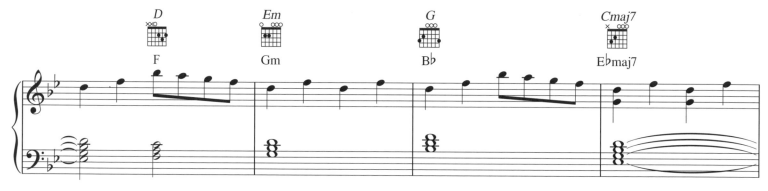

Once I was sev-en years old, my ma-ma told me, "Go make your-self some friends or you'll be lone-ly." ___ Once I was sev-en years

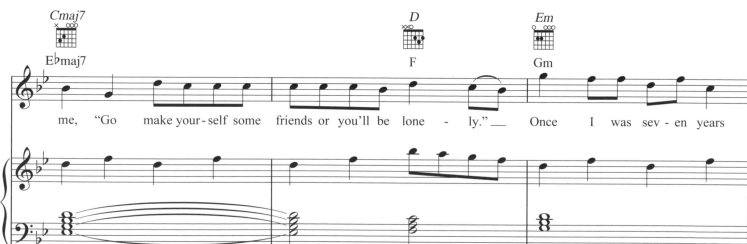

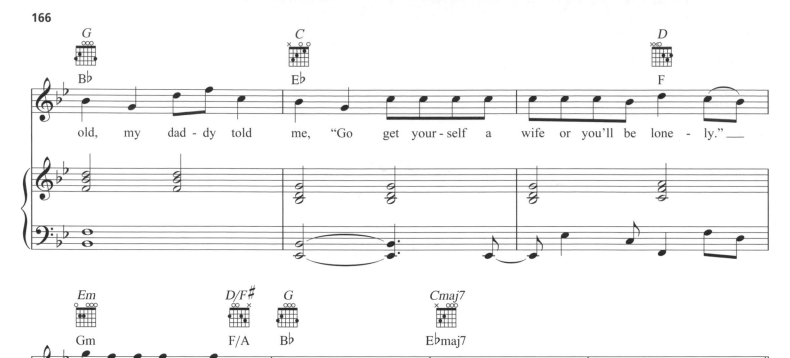

old, my dad-dy told me, "Go get your-self a wife or you'll be lone - ly." __

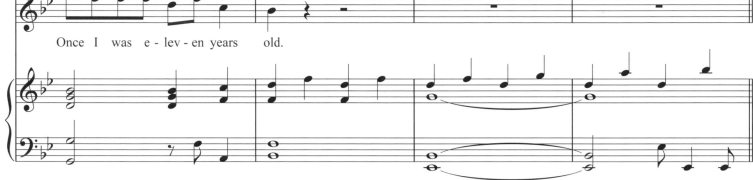

Once I was e - lev - en years old.

I al - ways had that __ dream __ like my dad - dy be - fore me,
I on - ly see my __ goals, __ I don't be - lieve __ in fail - ure

so I start - ed writ - ing songs, I start - ed writ - ing sto - ries.
'cause I know the small - est voic - es, they can make it ma - jor.

Once I was twen - ty years old.
Once I was twen - ty years old.

Soon we'll be thir - ty years

old. Our songs have been sold, we've trav-eled a-round the world and we're still roam - ing. __

Soon we'll be thir - ty years old.

Once I was sev-en years

old, my ma-ma told me, "Go make your-self some friends or you'll be lone - ly." __

Once I was sev-en years old.

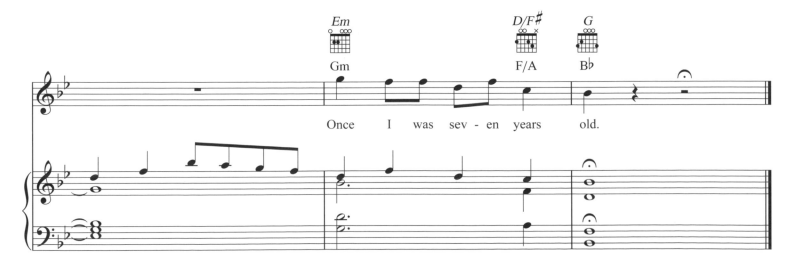

Once I was sev-en years old.

SHE WILL BE LOVED

Words and Music by ADAM LEVINE
and JAMES VALENTINE

SIGN OF THE TIMES

Words and Music by HARRY STYLES,
JEFF BHASKER, ALEX SALIBIAN,
TYLER JOHNSON, MITCH ROWLAND
and RYAN NASCI

Just stop your cry - ing; it's a sign of the times. _____
Just stop your cry - ing, have the time of your life. _____

Wel - come to the fi - nal show.   Hope you're wear - ing
Break - ing through the at - mos - phere,   and things are pret - ty

We got to, we got to, a - way. We

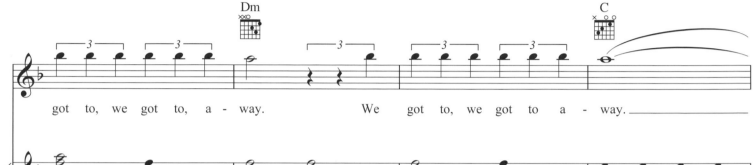

got to, we got to, a - way. We got to, we got to a - way.

SOMEONE LIKE YOU

Words and Music by ADELE ADKINS
and DAN WILSON

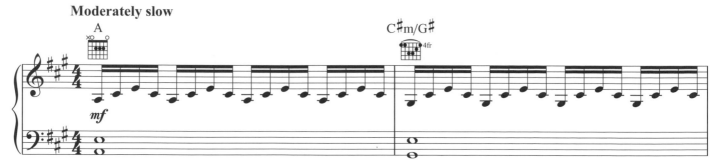

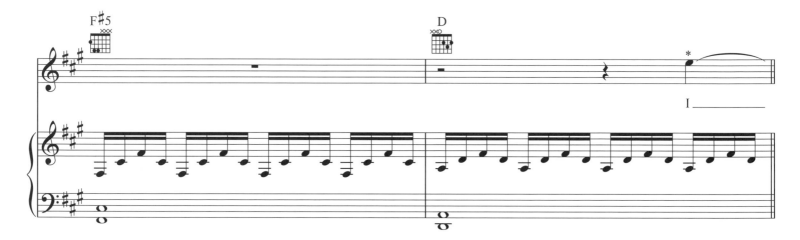

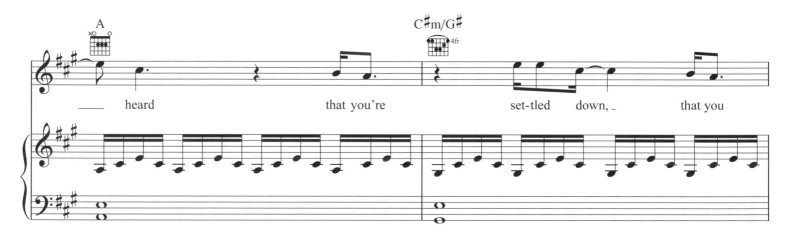

Vocal written one octave higher than originally sung.

I heard that your dreams came true. Guess she

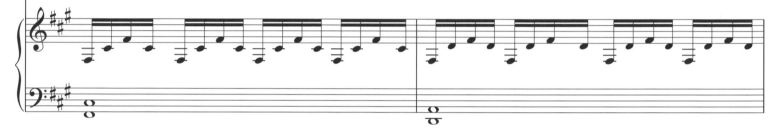

gave you things I did-n't give to you.

Old friend, why are you so shy? Ain't like

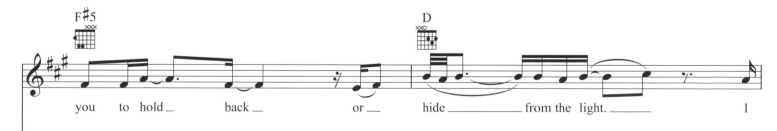

you to hold back or hide from the light. I

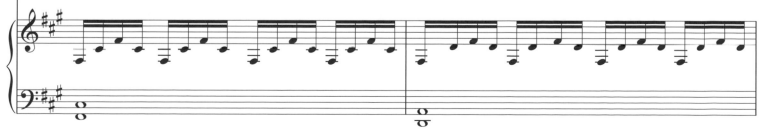

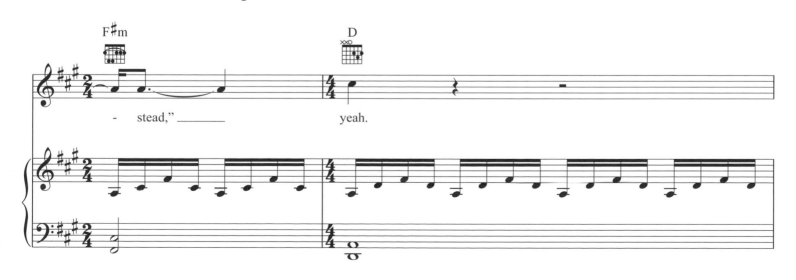

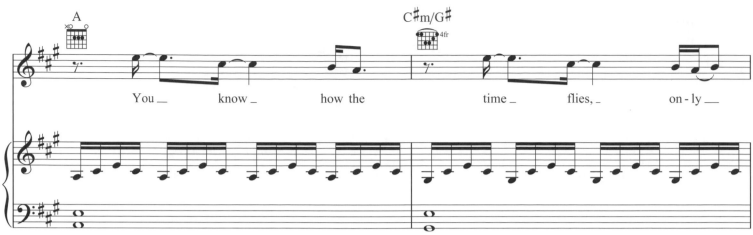

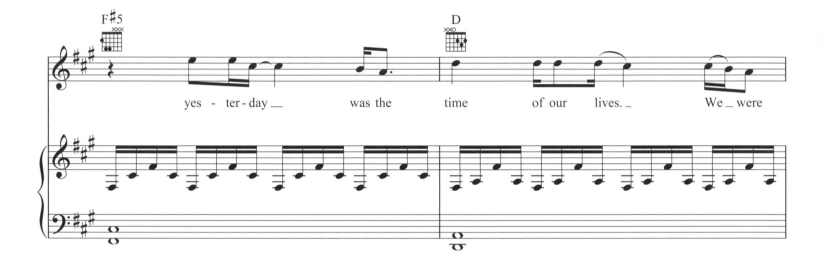

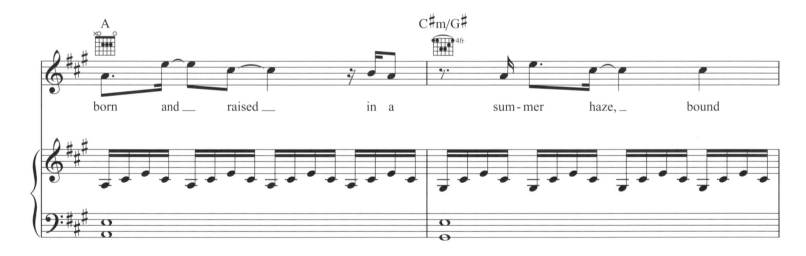

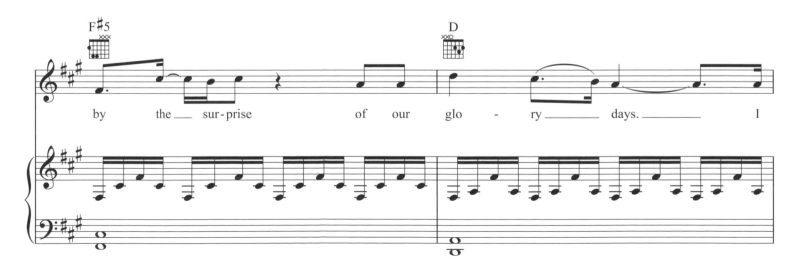

hate to turn up ___ out of the blue un-in-vit-ed, but I ___ could-n't stay a - way, ___ I could-n't fight it. I had

hoped you'd see my face ___ and that you'd be re-mind-ed that, for me, it is-n't o - ver. ___

___ Nev-er - mind, __ I'll find __ some-one like __

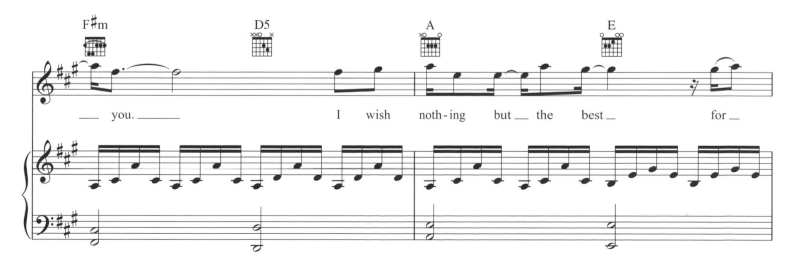

__ you. ___ I wish noth-ing but __ the best __ for __

lasts in love, but some-times it hurts in - stead. _____

Nev-er mind, _ I'll find _ some-one like _ you. _____ I wish

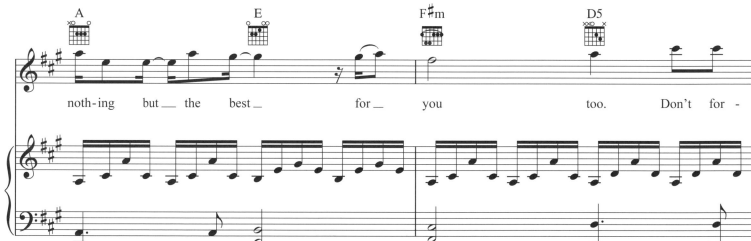

noth-ing but _ the best _ for _ you too. Don't for -

get me, I beg. _ I _ re - mem-ber _____ you said, _ "Some-times it

lasts in love, but some-times it hurts in - stead." _____ Some-times it

lasts in love, but some-times it hurts in - stead,

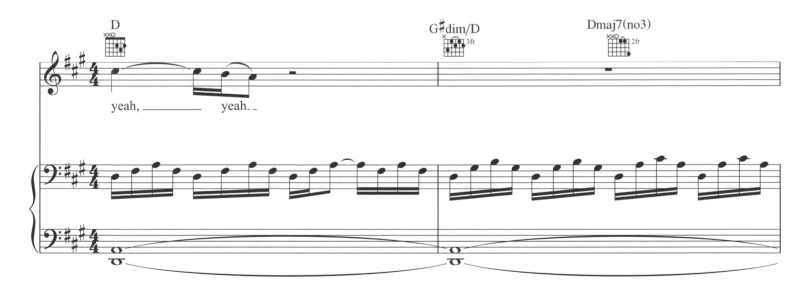

yeah, _____ yeah.

SOMEWHERE ONLY WE KNOW

Words and Music by TIM RICE-OXLEY,
RICHARD HUGHES and TOM CHAPLIN

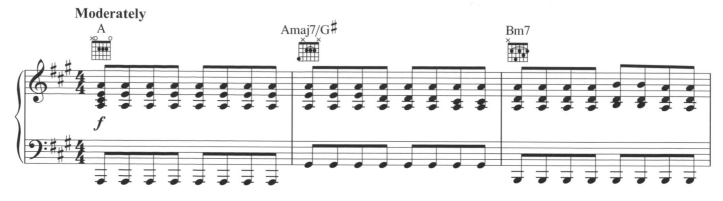

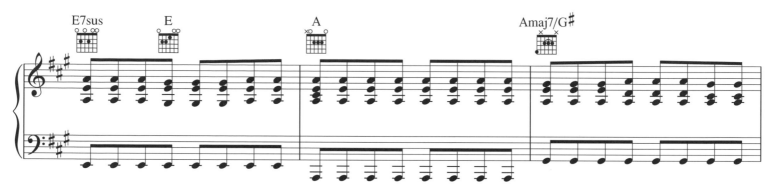

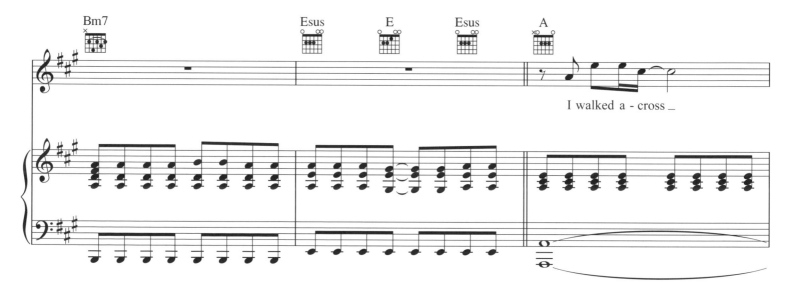

I walked a-cross _

an emp-ty land. _ I knew the path-way like the back of my hand. _

I came a-cross __ a fall - en __ tree. I felt the branch - es of it

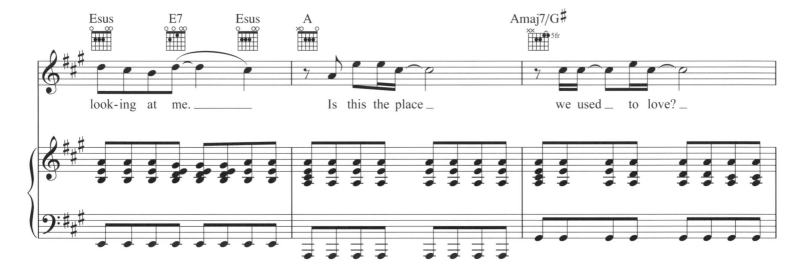

look-ing at me. __ Is this the place __ we used __ to love? __

Is this the place __ that I've __ been dream - ing of? __

Oh, sim - ple thing, __ where have you gone? __ I'm get-ting old and I need

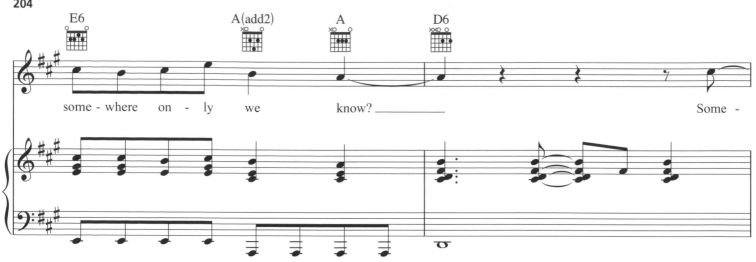

some - where on - ly we know? _____ Some -

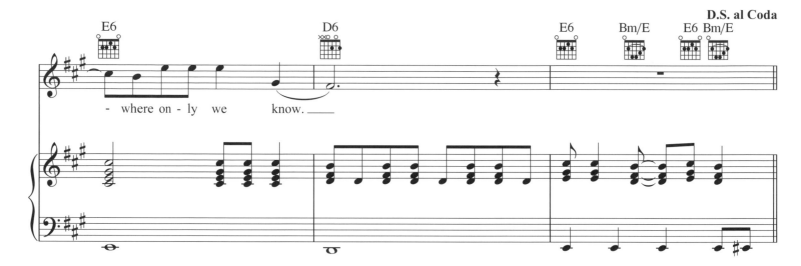

D.S. al Coda

- where on - ly we know. _____

CODA

So why don't we ___ go, so why don't we ___ go? _____

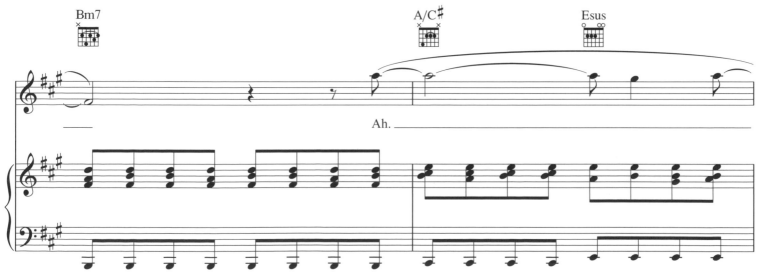

_____ Ah. _____

STAY WITH ME

Words and Music by SAM SMITH,
JAMES NAPIER, WILLIAM EDWARD PHILLIPS,
TOM PETTY and JEFF LYNNE

Guess it's true, I'm not good at a one-night stand.
Why am I so e-mo-tion-al?

But I still need love 'cause I'm just a man.
No, it's not a good look. Gain some self-con-trol.

These nights nev-er seem to go to plan.
And deep down I know this nev-er works.

Oh, won't you stay _____ with me? _____ 'Cause you're all _____ I need. _____ This ain't _

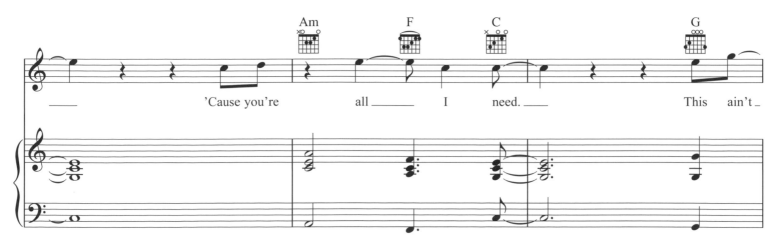

THINKING OUT LOUD

Words and Music by ED SHEERAN
and AMY WADGE

will __ be lov-ing you till __ we're sev-en-ty. ____
soul __ could nev-er grow old, __ it's ev-er-green. __

And ba-by, my heart could still feel as hard __ at twen-ty-three. __
And ba-by, your smile's for-ev-er in my mind __ and mem-o-ry. ____

And I'm think-ing 'bout how _____
And I'm think-ing 'bout how _____

peo-ple fall in love in mys-te-ri-ous ways, ____
peo-ple fall in love in mys-te-ri-ous ways, ____ and

(La, la, la, la, la, la, la, la, la, la, la, la.)

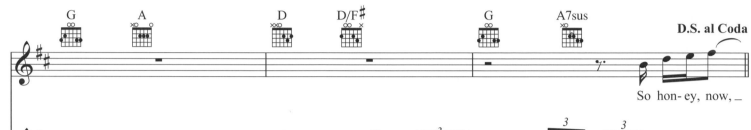

D.S. al Coda

So hon-ey, now, _

CODA

where we are. Ba - by, we found love right

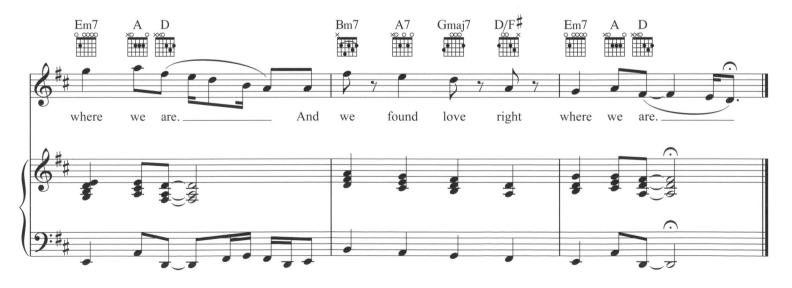

where we are. _____ And we found love right where we are. _____

A THOUSAND MILES

Words and Music by
VANESSA CARLTON

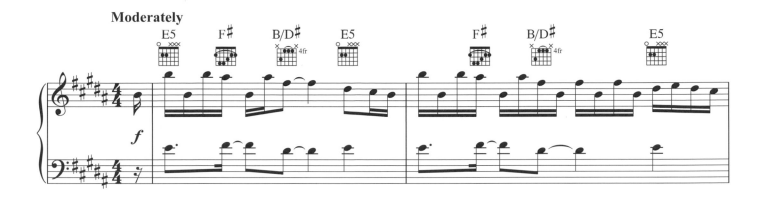

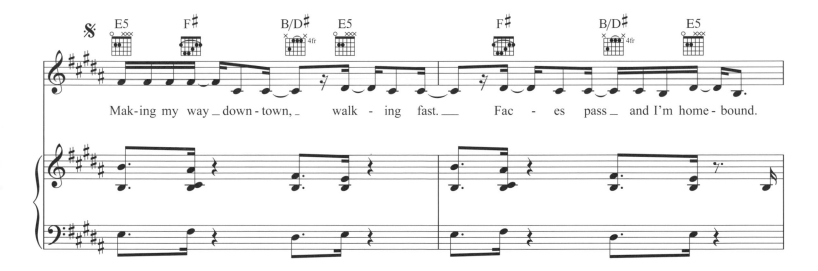

Mak-ing my way _ down-town, _ walk-ing fast. _ Fac - es pass _ and I'm home - bound.

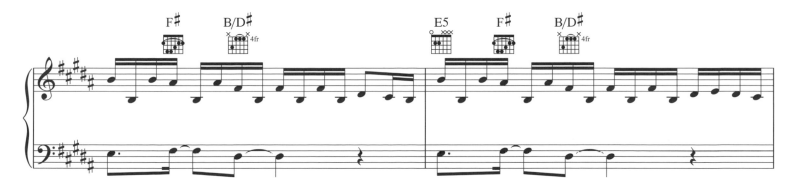

to the ___ sky, ___ do you think ___ time ___ would pass me ___ by? ___ 'Cause

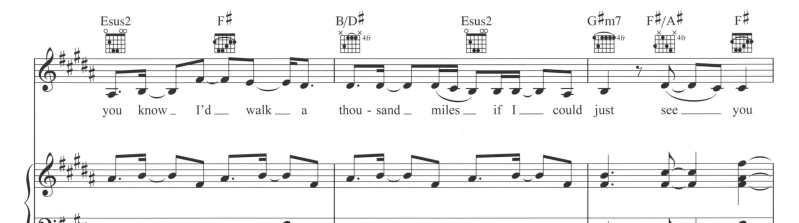

you know ___ I'd ___ walk ___ a thou - sand ___ miles ___ if I ___ could just see _____ you

to - night.   (1.) It's

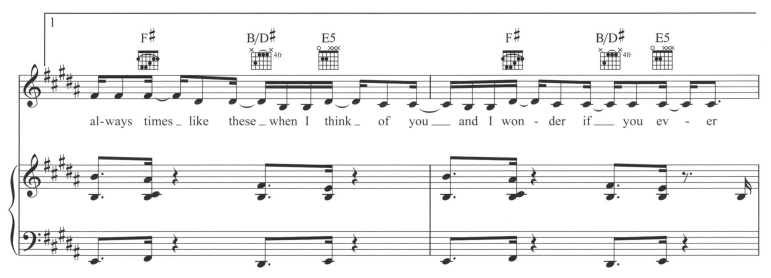

al - ways times ___ like these ___ when I think ___ of you ___ and I won - der if ___ you ev - er

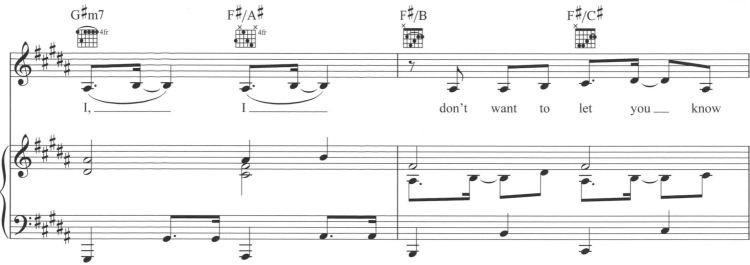

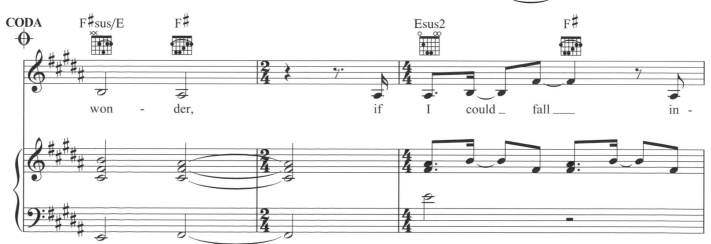

to the __ sky, __ do you think __ time __ would pass us __ by? 'Cause

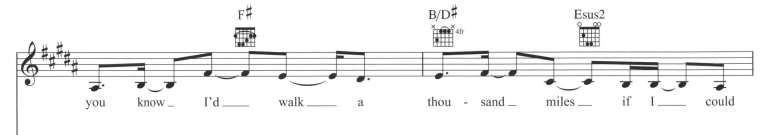

you know __ I'd __ walk __ a thou - sand __ miles __ if I __ could

just see ____ you. _____ If I could __ fall __ in -

to the __ sky, ____ do you think __ time __ would pass me __ by? ____ 'Cause

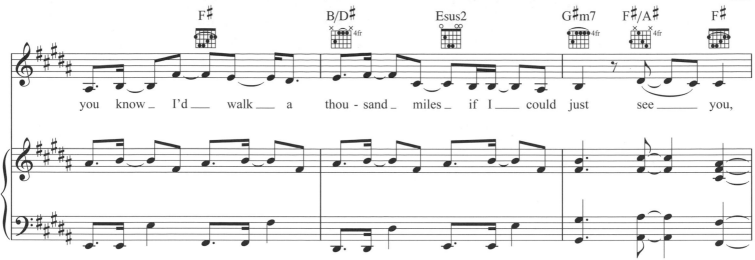

you know __ I'd __ walk __ a thou-sand __ miles __ if I __ could just __ see _____ you,

if I could just __ hold _____ you _____ to-

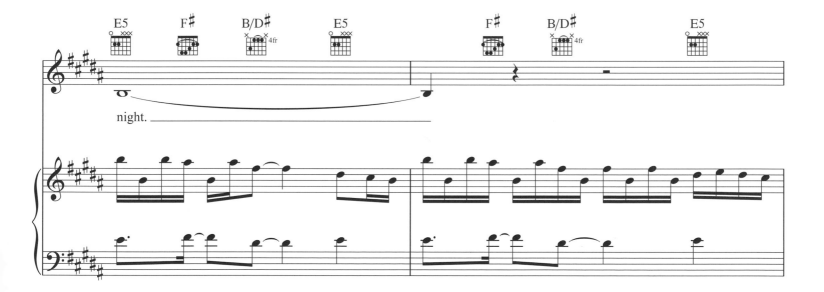

night. _____

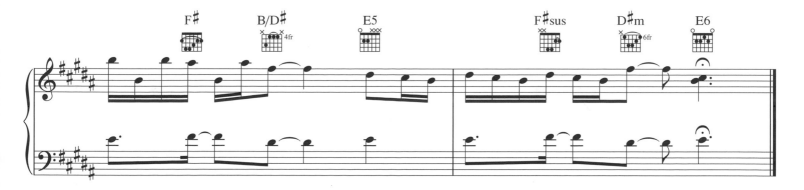

A THOUSAND YEARS

from the Summit Entertainment film THE TWILIGHT SAGA: BREAKING DAWN – PART 1

Words and Music by DAVID HODGES
and CHRISTINA PERRI

To Coda ⊕

I'll love you for ___ a thou - sand

more. ___

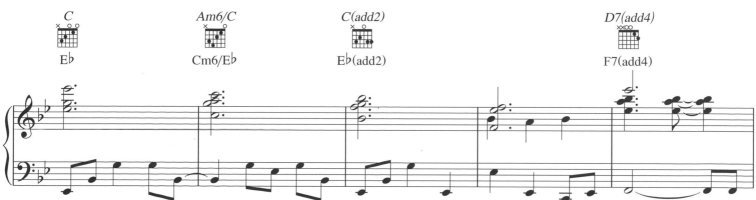

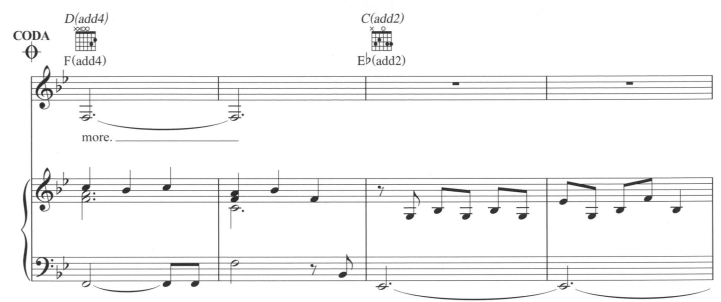

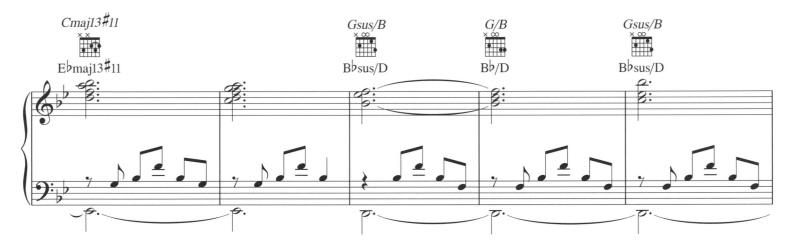

WHEN I WAS YOUR MAN

Words and Music by BRUNO MARS,
ARI LEVINE, PHILIP LAWRENCE
and ANDREW WYATT

Whether you're a karaoke singer or an auditioning professional, the **Pro Vocal®** series is for you! Unlike most karaoke packs, each book in the Pro Vocal series contains the lyrics, melody, and chord symbols for at least eight hit songs. The audio contains demos for listening, and separate backing tracks so you can sing along. Perfect for home rehearsal, parties, auditions, corporate events, and gigs without a backup band.

WOMEN'S EDITIONS

MEN'S EDITIONS

EXERCISES

MIXED EDITIONS

These editions feature songs for both male and female voices.

KIDS EDITIONS

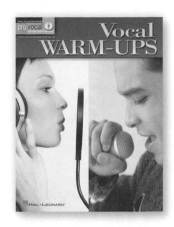

Visit Hal Leonard online at
www.halleonard.com

HAL•LEONARD®

Prices, contents, & availability subject to change without notice.

Disney Characters and Artwork
TM & © 2018 Disney